GAYLORD F

I'M NOT RAPPAPORT

I'M NOT RAPPAPORT

by Herb Gardner

NELSON DOUBLEDAY, INC., GARDEN CITY, NEW YORK

For Shel

I'M NOT RAPPAPORT was originally presented by the Seattle Repertory Theatre in December, 1984.

The play was subsequently presented by James Walsh, Lewis Allen, and Martin Heinfling at the American Place Theatre in New York City on June 6, 1985. The cast was as follows:

NAT	*Judd Hirsch*
MIDGE	*Cleavon Little*
DANFORTH	*Michael Tucker*
LAURIE	*Liann Pattison*
GILLEY	*Jace Alexander*
CLARA	*Cheryl Giannini*
THE COWBOY	*Ray Baker*

Directed by Daniel Sullivan. Setting by Tony Walton. Costumes by Robert Morgan. Lighting by Pat Collins.

This production was transferred to the Booth Theater in New York City on November 19, 1985 with the following cast:

NAT	*Judd Hirsch*
MIDGE	*Cleavon Little*
DANFORTH	*Gregg Almquist*
LAURIE	*Liann Pattison*
GILLEY	*Jace Alexander*
CLARA	*Mercedes Ruehl*
THE COWBOY	*Steve Ryan*

I'M NOT RAPPAPORT

CHARACTERS
NAT
MIDGE
DANFORTH
LAURIE
THE COWBOY
GILLEY
CLARA

SCENE
A bench near a path at the edge of the lake in Central Park; New York City, early October 1982.

ACT I: Three in the afternoon.

ACT II,   Scene 1:   Three in the afternoon, the next day.
          Scene 2:   Six in the evening, the next day.
          Scene 3:   Twelve days later, eleven in the morning.

Note: All stage directions and set descriptions are given from the audience's left and right.

Act One

SCENE: *A battered bench on an isolated path at the edge of Central Park Lake, early October, about three in the afternoon. To the left of this center bench is a smaller even more battered one with several of its slats missing. Behind these benches is the Gothic arch of an old stone tunnel, framed above by an ornate Romanesque bridge which spans the width of the stage.*

Before the curtain rises we hear the sound of a Carousel Band-Organ playing "The Queen City March."

AT RISE: *Two men, Midge and Nat, both about eighty years old, are seated at either end of the center bench; they sit several feet apart, an old briefcase between them. Midge is black and Nat is white. Midge wears very thick bifocals and an old soft hat; he is reading* The Sporting News. *Nat wears a beret and has a finely trimmed beard, a cane with an elegant ivory handle rests next to him against the bench. The two men do not look at each other. A Jogger runs by on the bridge above, exits at right. An autumn leaf or two drifts down through the late afternoon light. Silence for a few moments; only the now distant sound of the Carousel Music.*

NAT: O.K., where was I? *(No response. He smacks himself on the forehead)* Where the hell was I? What were we talking about? I was just about to make a very important point here. *(To Midge)* What were we talking about?

MIDGE: *(No response. He continues to read his newspaper for a moment)* We wasn't talking. *You* was talking. *(Turns page)* I wasn't talking.

NAT: O.K., so what was I saying?

MIDGE: I wasn't listening either. You was doing the whole thing by yourself.

NAT: Why weren't you listening?

MIDGE: Because you're a goddamn liar. I'm not listening to you anymore. Two days now I ain't been listening.

NAT: Stop pretending to read. You can't see anything.

MIDGE: Hey, how 'bout you go sit with them old dudes in fronta the Welfare Hotel, them old butter brains— *(Pointing about the lake)* the babies at the Carousel, them kids in the boat—or some o' them junkie-folk yonder, whyn't you go mess with them? 'Cause I'm not talking to you anymore, Mister. Puttin' you on notice of that. You may's well be talking to that tree over there.

NAT: It's a lamppost.

MIDGE: Sittin' here a week now, ain't heard a worda truth outa you. Shuckin' me every which way till the sun go down.

NAT: *(Slapping the bench)* I demand an explanation of that statement!

MIDGE: O.K., wise-ass; for example, are you or are you not an escaped Cuban terrorist?

NAT: *(Slapping the bench)* I am not!

MIDGE: O.K., and your name ain't Hernando—

NAT: Absolutely not!

MIDGE: So it's a lie—

NAT: It's a cover-story! *(Pause)* My line of work, they give you a cover-story.

MIDGE: Are you sayin'—?

NAT: All I'm saying, and that's *all* I'm saying, is that in my particular field you gotta have a cover-story. More than that I can't divulge at the present time.

MIDGE: Honey bun, you sayin' you're a spy?

NAT: I'm saying my name is Hernando and I'm an escaped Cuban terrorist.

MIDGE: But what kinda weirdo, bullshit cover-story is—?

NAT: You don't think I *said* that to them? That's what *I* said to them. I said to them, an eighty-one-year-old Lithuanian is a Cuban Hernando? That's right, they said, tough luck, sweetheart; yours is not to reason why. That's how they talk. Of *course* you don't believe it! You think *I* believe it? Such dopes. But it's a living. I beg you not to inquire further.

MIDGE: But why'd they pick an old—

NAT: Do *I* know? You tell *me.* A year ago I'm standing in line at the Medicaid, a fellah comes up to me— boom, I'm an undercover.

MIDGE: *(Impressed)* Lord . . .

NAT: Who knows, maybe they got something. They figure an old man, nobody'll pay attention. Could wander through the world like a ghost, pick up some tidbits.

MIDGE: *(Nodding thoughtfully)* Yeah . . .

NAT: So maybe they got something, even though, I grant you, they screwed up on the cover-story. All I know is every month a thousand bingos is added to my Social Security check.

MIDGE: Bingos?

NAT: Bingos. Dollars. Cash. It's a word we use in the business. Please don't inquire further. *(Silence)* Please, I'm not at liberty. *(Longer silence)* O.K.; they also gave me a code name, "Harry."

MIDGE: "Harry?

NAT: Harry Schwartzman.

MIDGE: What's your real name?

NAT: Sam Schwartzman. *(Outraged)* Can you believe it? Can you *believe* it? That's some imaginative *group* they got up there, right? That's some bunch of geniuses! *(Then, shrugging)* What the hell, a thousand bananas on your Social Security every month you don't ask fancy questions.

MIDGE: Best not, best not. *(Leaning closer)* So, do ya . . . do ya ever pick up any information for them?

NAT: Are you kidding? Sitting on a bench all day with a man who can't tell a tree from a lamppost? Not a shred. *(Glances about, leans closer)* Fact is, I think they got me in what they call "deep cover." See, they keep you in this "deep cover" for years; like five, maybe ten years they keep you there, till you're just like this regular person in the neighborhood . . . and then, boom, they pick you out for the big one. Considering my age and general health, they're not too bright. *(Reaches into briefcase)* O.K., snack time.

MIDGE: *(Nodding)* Yeah. Deep cover. I hearda that . . .

NAT: *(Taking foil-wrapped sandwich from briefcase)* Here. Tuna salad with lettuce and tomato on whole wheat toast. Take half.

MIDGE: *(Accepting sandwich)* Thank ya, Sam; thank ya.

NAT: Yeah, comes three o'clock, there's nothing like a nice, fresh tuna salad sandwich.

MIDGE: *(Chewing)* Uh-huh.

NAT: *(Chewing)* Crisp.

(Silence for a moment as they eat their sandwiches)

MIDGE: *(Suddenly)* Bullshit! *(Sits upright)* Bullshit! Lord, you done it to me *again!* You done it! *(Throws the sandwich fiercely to the ground)* Promised myself I wouldn't let ya, and ya done it again! Deep cover! Harry Schwartzman! Bingos! You done it again!

NAT: *(Smiling to himself as he continues eating)* That was nice . . . a nice long story, lasted a long time . . .

MIDGE: *(Shouting, poking Nat sharply)* That's *it!* That's it, no more conversin'! Conversin' is *over* now, Mister! No more, ain't riffin' *me* no more!

NAT: Please control yourself—

MIDGE: *Move* it, boy; *away* with ya! This here's *my* spot!

NAT: Sir, I was—

MIDGE: This is *my* spot. I come here first!

NAT: I was merely—

MIDGE: Get offa my spot 'fore I lay you out!

NAT: *Your* spot? Who made it *your* spot? Show me the plaque. Where does it say that?

MIDGE: Says right here . . . *(Remains seated, slowly circling his fists in the air like a boxer)* You read them hands? Study them hands, boy. Them hands were Golden Gloves, summer of Nineteen and Twenty-Four. This here's *my* spot, *been* my spot six months now, my good and peaceful spot till you show up a week ago, start playin' Three Card Monte with my head. Want you *gone*, Sonny! *(Continues circling his fists)* Givin' ya three t'make dust; comin' out on the count o'three. *One—*

(Midge rises, moving to his corner of the "ring")

NAT: Wait, a brief discussion—

MIDGE: Sound of the bell, I'm comin' out. *You* won't hear it but I *will. Two—*

NAT: How you gonna hit me if you can't *see* me?

MIDGE: Dropped Billy D'Amato in the sixth round with both eyes swole shut. I just keep punchin' till I hear crunchin'. *Three!*

NAT: *(Rising, with dignity)* Please, sir—this is an embarrassing demonstration—

MIDGE: *(Moving in Nat's general direction, a bit of remembered footwork, jabbing)* O.K., comin' out, comin' out; comin' at ya, boy, comin' at ya—

NAT: *(Moving behind bench for protection)* Sir, you
. . . you have a depressing personality and a terrible
attitude!

MIDGE: *Prepare* yourself, Mister, prepare yourself, get
your—

*(Midge suddenly lunges, bumping against the bench,
stumbling—he struggles to keep his balance, grabbing
desperately at the air—then falls flat on his back in the
path. He lies there silently for several moments)*

MIDGE: *(Quietly, frightened)* Oh, shit . . .

NAT: *(Aware that Midge is in danger, whispering)* Mister . . . ? *(No response. He leans forward urgently)*
Mister, Mister . . . ? *(Silence. He moves toward
Midge as quickly as possible)* Don't move, don't
move . . .

MIDGE: *(Trembling)* I know . . .

NAT: Could be you broke something . . .

MIDGE: *(Softly)* I know. Oh, shit. Never fall down,
never fall down . . .

NAT: *(Kneeling next to him, trying to calm him)* It's
nothing; I fall down every morning. I get up, I have a
cup of coffee, I fall down. That's the system; two years
old you stand up and then, boom, seventy years later
you fall down again. *(Gently, firmly)* O.K., first thing;
can you lift your head? *(Midge hesitates, frightened,
then raises his head a bit)* Good sign. Put your head

back. *(As Midge carefully rests his head back)* Good, good, good . . . *(Carefully, knowledgeably, touching Midge, checking for damage)* O.K., feeling for breaks, checking the pelvic area . . . feeling the hip now . . . If you like this we're engaged. *(Midge moans softly, frightened)* Don't worry; breaks is also nothing. Everybody breaks. Me, I got a hip like a teacup. Twice last year; I just got rid of my walker. *(Continues checking Midge's left leg; Midge winces)* I was also dead once for a while. Six minutes. Also nothing; don't worry. They're doing a bypass, everything stops; they had to jump-start me like a Chevrolet. *(Starts checking Midge's right leg. Midge apprehensive)* Six minutes dead, the doctor said. You know what it's like? Boring. First thing you float up and stick to the ceiling like a kid's balloon, you look around. Down below on the bed there's a body you wouldn't give a nickel for. It's you. Meanwhile you're up on the ceiling; nobody sees you. Not bad for a while, nice; you meet some other dead guys, everybody smiles, you hear a little music; but mostly boring. *(He has finished checking Midge's legs)* O.K.; can you move your arms? *(Midge demonstrates a few, short boxing jabs)* Excellent. O.K., good news: each item functional. Now, from experience, lie there and relax five minutes before you get up. *(Midge murmurs obediently)* O.K., best thing for relaxing is jokes—*(Rising to center bench near him)* Willy Howard, you hearda him? The best. O.K., years ago he had this great routine, see—

MIDGE: That was another lie, wasn't it?

NAT: What?

MIDGE: 'Bout you bein' dead.

NAT: A *fact,* that was an absolute—

MIDGE: Man, you ain't even *friendly* with the truth! *Lies.* Goddamn *lies! (Slaps the ground)* It's your goddamn lies put me on the canvas here! Got me fightin', fallin' down—

NAT: *Not* lies— *(Sits upright on bench)* Alterations! I make certain alterations. Sometimes the truth don't fit; I take in here, I let out there, till it fits. The *truth?* What's true is a triple bypass last year at Lenox Hill, what's true is Grade Z cuts of meat from the A and P, a Social Security check that wouldn't pay the rent for a chipmunk; what's true is going to the back door of the Plaza Hotel every morning for yesterday's clubrolls, I tell them it's for the pigeons. I'm the pigeon. Six minutes dead is *true*— *(Takes bunch of pages from briefcase)* here, Dr. Reissman's bills; here's the phone number, call him. A fact. And that was my *last* fact. Since then, alterations. Since I died, a new policy! This morning I tell the counterman at Walgreen's I'm an American Indian. An Iroquois. He listens; next thing I know I'm remembering the old days on the plains, the broken treaties, my Grandpa fighting the cavalry. Not important he's convinced; *I* am, and I love it. I was one person for eighty-one years, why not a hundred for the next five?!

MIDGE: *(After a moment, resting on his elbows, thoughtfully)* Them club-rolls; how early you figure a fellah oughta show up down there to—

NAT: *Rolls, rolls;* you missed the whole *point—*

MIDGE: *(Rising carefully to small bench)* The *point?* I *got* the point; the point is you're crazy, the point is you ain't never seein' your marbles again!

NAT: Ah, how fortunate, an expert on mental health. My daughter Clara, she's another expert— *(Holds up one of the pages)* here, wants to put me in a home for the ridiculous. "No sense of reality," she writes, "in need of supervision," she writes. This she writes to my therapist, Dr. Engels. Trouble is I don't have a therapist and I'm Dr. Engels. I give her the address of the Young Socialists' Club on Eighty-Sixth; I'm listed there as Doctor Friedrich Engels. *(Leans closer to him)* Crazy, you say? Listen to me, listen to Dr. Engels. You're a wreck. Look at you; is this who you want to be? Is this what you had in mind for old, this guy here? A man who obviously passed away some time ago? Whatta you got left, five minutes, five months? Is this how you want to spend it? Sitting and staring, once in a while for a thrill falling down? *(Urgently)* No, *wrong;* you gotta shake things *up,* fellah; you gotta make things *happen—*

MIDGE: *(Truly outraged) Hold* it now! Hold that mouth right there! You tellin' *me* how to live? *You* tellin' *me?* You talkin' to an *em*-ployed person here, Mister! *(Retrieving his newspaper from Nat's bench, returning with great dignity to his own)* Midge Carter; you talkin' to Midge Carter here, boy—Super-in-tendent in charge of Three Twenty-One Central Park West; *run* the place, *been* runnin' it forty-two years, July. They got a furnace been there long as *I* have—an ol'

Erie City Special, fourteen *tonner,* known to *kill* a man don't show he's boss. Buildin' don't move without that bull and that bull don't move without *me.* Don't have to make up nobody to be when I *am* somebody! *(Settling himself proudly on small bench)* Shake things up, huh? Don't shake *nothin'* up. How you figure I keep my job? Near fifteen years past retirement, how you figure I'm still super there? I ain't mentioned a raise in fifteen years, and they ain't neither. Moved to the nightshift three years ago, outa the public eye. Daytime a buncha A-rab Supers has come and gone, not Midge. Dozen Spic Doormen dressed up like five-star generals, come and gone, not Midge. Mister, you lookin' at the wise old invisible man.

NAT: No, I'm looking at a dead man! *(Points cane at him)* Fifteen years, no raise; it's a dead person, a ghost! You let them rob you!

MIDGE: They don't rob me; *nobody* robs me, got a system. You see that boy come every day, five o'clock? That's Gilley; give him three bucks, nobody robs me. Ten blocks from here to my place, walks me there, protects me.

NAT: From who?

MIDGE: Him, for one. Fifteen a week, he don't rob me —but nobody *else* neither, see; now *that's* Social Security—

NAT: *(Laughing)* Oh, God—

MIDGE: Keep chucklin', sugar; ain't nobody dyin' of old age in *this* neighborhood.

NAT: Job! I see what your *job* is. Groveling! You're a licensed groveler!

MIDGE: *(Rises from bench, shouting)* Super at Three Twenty-One, still got a *callin'*—only thing people got to call *you* is "hey, old man!"

NAT: What do *you* know? What does a *ghost* know? *(Rising proudly)* People *see* me; they *see* me! I *make* them see me! *(His cane in the air)* The night they rushed me to Lenox Hill for the bypass, as they carried me out on the *stretcher,* six tenants called the Landlord to see if my apartment was available. Now, every *day*, every day at dawn I ring their bells, all six of them—the door opens, I holler "Good morning, Vulture; Four B is still unavailable!" I hum the first two bars of "The Internationale" and walk away.

MIDGE: *(Moving toward him)* Old *fool*, crazy old fool; they can't see *you.* They can hear ya, but they sure can't *see* ya. Don't want to *look* at your old face; mine neither—I just help 'em out. Don't you get it, baby?— *both* of us ghosts only *you* ain't noticed. We old and not rich and done the sin of leavin' slow. No use to fight it, you go with it or you break, boy, 'specially bones like *we* got.

NAT: *(Shouting)* Traitor! Traitor in the ranks! It's people like you give old a bad name—

DANFORTH'S VOICE: *(Shouting)* Carter—

NAT: It's *your* type that—

DANFORTH'S VOICE: Carter—*(Peter Danforth enters on the bridge, Up Left, jogging; he is the same man who ran by earlier. Danforth is in his early forties and wears a newly purchased jogging outfit)* Carter . . . ah, good, *there* you are, Carter . . .

MIDGE: *(Glancing about, not sure who it is or where the voice is coming from)* Midge Carter, here I am.

DANFORTH: *(Slowing his pace)* Here, up here . . . on the bridge . . . *(Jogging in place, cordially)* Danforth . . . Peter Danforth, Twelve H . . .

MIDGE: *(Squinting up)* Danforth, right . . .

DANFORTH: *(Breathlessly)* Been looking for you—several days now—they told me you might be in this area—our meeting, remember?

MIDGE: Our meetin', yeah . . .

DANFORTH: How about right here, soon as I finish my run?

MIDGE: Right here, you got it.

DANFORTH: Be right with you . . . *(Quickening his pace again)* Three more miles, be right with you, Carter; looking forward to it . . .

MIDGE: *(Shouting up, as Danforth exits right)* Lookin' forward to the meetin', yessir; been on my schedule

. . . *(Suddenly whispering, terrified)* Oh shit, the Man, the Man, he found me—

NAT: What man?

MIDGE: *The* Man, *the* Man, been duckin' him, he *found* me.

NAT: *What* man? What is it, Carter?

MIDGE: *(Sits on center bench, trembling, brushing off clothes, adjusting hat, trying to pull himself together)* Mr. Danforth, Twelve H, Head o' the Tenants' Committee. Place is goin' Co-op, he says they got some reorganizin' to do, says he wants to see me private . . .

NAT: *(Softly, nodding)* Ah, yes . . .

MIDGE: Last fellah wanted to see me private was when they found my wife Daisy under the Seventy-Ninth Street Crosstown. *(Buttoning sweater, trying for a bit of dignity)* See, problem is, it's been gettin' around the buildin' that I'm kinda nearsighted—

NAT: *(Sitting next to him)* Nearsighted? Helen *Keller* was *near*sighted.

MIDGE: Got the place memorized, see. But last week I'm in the basement, lady from Two A sees me walk right smack into the elevator door. Mrs. Carsten, Two A, she's standin' in the laundry room watchin' me. Figured I'd fake her out, so I do it *again*, like I was *meanin'* to do it, like it's this *plan* I got to walk into the elevator door—dumb, dumb, *knowed* it was a dumb move while I was *doin'* it. Just kept slammin' into that elevator door till she went away. I'm shoutin', "gonna have this thing fixed in a jiffy, Mrs. Carsten!" Next thing I know Danforth wants to see me private. *(Hits himself on the head)* Panicked on the *ropes* is what I did; that's what blew it for me in the ring too . . .

(Silence for a moment)

NAT: *(Quietly)* Are the cataracts in both eyes?

MIDGE: *(After a moment; quietly)* Yeah.

NAT: How many times removed?

MIDGE: Left twice, the right once. But they come back.

NAT: That's what they do. They're dependable. And how bad is the glaucoma?

MIDGE: Drops an' pills keep it down. 'Cept night-times. Night-times—

NAT: Night-times it's like you're trying to close your lid over a basketball.

MIDGE: No lie. No *lie.* When'd it start with you? Start with me four, five years back; nothin' on the sides. No p'ripheral vision, doc says. Five years back—*(He waves)* So long, p'ripheral vision. Then one mornin' there's this spot in the middle . . .

NAT: Ah, the spot, the spot . . .

MIDGE: Like the moon, this dead pearly spot . . .

NAT: The moon exactly . . .

MIDGE: And it gets to growin' . . .

NAT: Oh, yes . . .

MIDGE: Then, thank the Lord, it stops. Then what you got is the pearly moon spot, no p'ripherals, and this ring between 'em where folks come in and out.

NAT: Exactly; like birds. *(Leans close to him)* You get color or black and white?

MIDGE: Mostly blue. Blue shadows like. Weird thing is, all my dreams is still in full color, see everything real sharp and clear like when I was young—then I wake up and it's real life looks like a dream.

NAT: Exactly! Same with me *exactly!* I hadn't thought about it till this minute! *(His arm around Midge)* Carter, we're connected. Why? Because we both got vision. Who needs sight when we got vision! Connected! Yes, even with your cowardly personality and your chicken-shit attitude. Yes, I'm sure now. Our meeting with Danforth will go well, I'm convinced.

MIDGE: *Our* meetin'? What—

NAT: Yes, I have decided to handle this Danforth matter for you. Don't worry. The Exploiters, the Land Owners, the Capitalist Fat Cats, I eat them for lunch.

MIDGE: *(Alarmed)* Hold on now, boy, I never asked—

NAT: Don't thank me. I ask for nothing in return, only to see justice. Don't thank *me;* thank Karl Marx, thank Lenin, thank Gorky, thank Olgin—

MIDGE: Hey, don't need *none* o' you guys—

NAT: But mostly thank Ben Gold; in Nineteen-Nineteen I join the Communist Party and the human race and meet Ben Gold. *He's* the one, *that* was vision— *(As Midge starts to edge away from him on the bench)* Ben Gold, who organized the Fur Workers and gave them a heart and a center and a voice! What a voice, you thought it was yours. I'm matching skins at Supreme Furs, he makes me Assistant Shop Chairman; I'm at his side when we win. A ten percent wage increase and the first forty-hour week in the city! We win! *(Bangs his cane on the ground)* Where is he? Where is Danforth? Bring him to me. Bring me the Fascist four-flusher!

MIDGE: *(Softly, covering his face)* Oh my God . . .

NAT: *(Turns to answer Midge)* O.K., O.K., the Soviet Union, throw it up to me; everybody does. They screwed up, I'm the first one to admit it. I promise you, Carter, they lost me, *finished.* I gave up on them . . . but I never gave up on the ideas. The triumph of the proletariat, a workers' democracy, the ideas are still fine and beautiful, the ideas go on, they are better than the people who had them. Ben Gold, they hit him with the Taft-Hartley and the fire goes out, but the voice goes on; the conflict goes on like the turning

of the stars and we will crush Danforth before sup-
pertime.

*(Nat taps his cane with finality; sits back, crosses his
legs, waiting for his adversary. Midge is silent for a
moment. Then he turns to Nat, quietly, calmly)*

MIDGE: You done now? You finished talkin'? *(Nat nods,
not looking at him)* O.K., listen to me; Danforth
comes, don't want you speakin'. Not a word. Not one
word. Don't even want you here. Got it? You open
your face once, I'm gonna give Gilley ten bucks to
nail you permanent. Got that? Am I comin' through
clear?

NAT: *(Turns to Midge, smiling graciously)* Too late. I
have no choice. I'm obligated. The conflict between
me and Danforth is inevitable. I am obligated to get
you off your knees and into the sunlight.

MIDGE: No you ain't. Lettin' you outa that obligation
right now. *(Leans toward Nat, urgently)* Please, it's
O.K., I got it all worked out what to say to him. Just
gotta hang in till I get my Christmas tips, see—they
only got to keep me three more months till Christmas
and I'll be—

NAT: Christmas! Compromises! How do you think we
lost Poland? Danforth has no right! The man has no
right to dismiss you before your time—

MIDGE: Man, I'm eighty-*one*—

NAT: And when we finish with *him,* at five o'clock we'll take care of the hoodlum, Gilley. Together we'll teach *that* punk a lesson!

MIDGE: *(Looks up at the sky, desperately)* Why, Lord? Why are you doing this to me? Lord, I asked you for help and you sent me a weird Commie blind man . . .

NAT: What Lord? Who is this Lord you're talking to? Oh *boy,* I can see I've got a lot of work to do here . . .

MIDGE: *(Turning sharply up right)* Shit, here he comes, the Man comin' now . . .

NAT: *(Turning up right)* Ah, good, I'm ready . . .

MIDGE: *(Grips Nat's arm)* Please, baby; I'm askin' ya, please be quiet—

NAT: Calm down, Carter—

MIDGE: Never done you no harm—

NAT: It's not him anyway. *(Leans to right, peering up at bridge)* No, definitely not him. It's a pretty girl.

MIDGE: How do you know?

NAT: Because of the glow. When I could see, all pretty girls had a glow. Now what's left is the glow. That's how you can tell.

(Laurie enters Up Right on the bridge, and she is a pretty girl—soft, delicate, innocent, about twenty-five,

wearing a dress to match the gentle October day. Carrying a large sketchpad and a box of charcoals, she crosses to an old stone ledge beneath a lamppost at the far left side of the bridge, unaware of Midge and Nat, who are some distance below her. Once at the ledge she closes her eyes and breathes deeply, inhaling the view of the lake; then she settles herself on the ledge and proceeds briskly, studiously, to sketch the view—all this as Midge and Nat continue their dialogue)

NAT: Yes, definitely; a pretty girl . . .

MIDGE: *(Rising urgently from bench)* Maybe so, but the Man comin' *soon—(Pulling Nat to his feet)* time for the *Man,* time for you to *go—*

NAT: Calm down, Carter, you're hysterical—

MIDGE: *(Moving Nat away from bench)* Ain't you got an appointment someplace? Whyn't you go tell somebody you're an Apache—

NAT: *(With genuine concern)* All right, all right, *you* will handle Danforth; I will permit it.

MIDGE: Good—

NAT: But first you must calm yourself—

MIDGE: I'll calm myself—

NAT: This is essential. In your present state the Land Baron will walk all over you; I cannot allow that. Here, this will do the trick— *(Reaches quickly into his jacket pocket, withdrawing small brown business envelope)* Here, some government grass to relax you. Official, legal; dope from Uncle Sam. The doctor prescribes, the government pays; two ounces a month for the glaucoma. Dilates the capillaries, relieves the pressure; everywhere. *(Takes a joint from the envelope)* Here. All rolled. Be my guest. Medicaid is paying.

MIDGE: *(Peering anxiously off right)* Better not; makes me foolish sometimes. Ain't no time to get foolish—

NAT: Not foolish. Happy. I promise, you'll laugh at the Six O'Clock News. Even your children become amusing. *(Lights joint, inhales, hands it out to Midge)* Please, calm yourself. Here, take a hit, Danforth will be a piece of cake; one puff, the man is a Danish.

MIDGE: *(Still very much on guard)* You swear you'll keep your mouth shut when the Man comes, shut *tight*—I'll take a puff.

NAT: Here, direct from the White House. *(Midge hesitates a moment; then takes a deep drag)* Good; now hold it in as long as you—

MIDGE: I know, I know; I was smokin' dope while you was eatin' Matzoh-balls, baby. *(Another deep drag, hands it back to Nat)* Fair stuff. Just fair.

(The distant sound of the Carousel Band-Organ begins off left as though carried on the autumn breeze. Laurie looks up from her sketching for a moment, smiles, hearing the gently drifting melody of "That Old Gang of

Mine." Midge and Nat will pass the joint back and forth between them as their dialogue continues, the grass gradually starting to reach them)

MIDGE: *(Glancing anxiously up right)* Man say three miles, he sure takin' it slow.

NAT: Maybe he dropped dead. *(On the inhale, handing joint to Midge)* A lot of these running people; boom.

MIDGE: *(On the inhale)* Young fellah like him?

NAT: They're the first ones; the young ones. Boom. They're running, they're smiling; boom. You should be here in the evening, they drop like flies . . . *(Chuckling, taking joint from Midge)* Boom, boom, boom . . . *(Midge chuckles along with him, Nat studies the joint fondly for a moment)* All my life I fought for socialized medicine . . .

MIDGE: Stopped smoking dope when I turned seventy . . .

NAT: *(Peering up at Laurie)* That girl just went from very pretty to beautiful . . .

MIDGE: Scared of goin' foolish. My Daddy went foolish five years before he died, didn't know his own name. Sad to see. Hope I ain't the only one hearin' that music.

NAT: *(Moving toward bench, squinting up at Laurie)* Now she's Hannah Pearlman . . .

MIDGE: Who?

NAT: *(Sits on bench; softly)* Hannah Pearlman. She worked as a Finisher, stitched linings for yachting caps, Shiffman's Chapeaux on West Broadway. Nineteen Twenty-One.

MIDGE: *(Joins Nat at bench; squints up at Laurie for a moment)* No, ain't her. Tell you who you got there; that's Ella Mae Tilden . . .

(Both looking up at Laurie as they talk, getting more and more stoned; the gentle Carousel Music continuing, bringing the past with it on the breeze. Now, in this delicate, dappled, late-afternoon light, Laurie truly seems to have the glow that Nat described)

NAT: Very shy, shyer even than me. She would sit on her stoop in the early evening, a fine, fine face like an artist would paint . . .

MIDGE: Ella Mae; best wife I had, number three. Five all told. It's Ella Mae give me John, it's John give me Billy, and it's Billy give me these teeth . . .

NAT: I passed that stoop a million times; I couldn't say hello. Funny-looking fingers from the stitching, she sat on the stoop with her hands hidden, like so . . .

MIDGE: Eight grandchildren professionals and Billy's the dentist. Billy give me this smile *(He demonstrates)* Put the teeth in, smiled, and left Ella Mae. Smile needed a new hat, and the hat made me walk a new way, which was out . . .

NAT: Also she was married. Yeah, went to work so her greenhorn husband could go to law school, become an American Somebody. Comes June, Arnold Pearlman graduates, suddenly finds out he's an attorney with a Yiddish-speaking wife who finishes yachting caps. Boom; he leaves her for a smooth-fingered Yankee Doodle he met at school. Four months later Hannah took the gas; a popular expression at that time for putting your head in an oven . . .

MIDGE: Poor Ella Mae cryin', me hearin' my new mouth say goodbye. She was near seventy then, but when my mind moves to her she is fresh peach prime . . .

NAT: September, a month before she took the gas, I see her in the Grand Street Library, second-floor reading room. A special place, quiet, not even a clock; I'm at the main table with *Macbeth*. I look up, there's Hannah Pearlman. She doesn't see me; her head is buried in a grammar book for a ten-year-old. She looks up, she knows me, she smiles. My heart goes directly into my ears, bang, bang, bang, I'm deaf. I don't speak. I can't speak. I'm there in the house of words; I can't speak. She puts her hands under the table, goes back to her book. After a while she leaves. I didn't *speak* . . .

MIDGE: *(Bangs his fist on the bench)* Goddamn smile got me two more wives and nothin' but trouble! Damn these teeth and damn my wanderin' ways . . . *(Takes out huge handkerchief; the Carousel Music fades)*

NAT: I didn't *speak*, I didn't *speak* . . .

MIDGE: *(Blowing his nose)* There's dope makes you laugh and dope makes you cry. I think this here's cryin' dope.

NAT: *(Bangs his cane on the ground)* Stop, stop! Nostalgia, I hate it! The dread disease of old people! Kills more of us than heart failure!

MIDGE: *(Drying his eyes)* When's the last time you made love to a woman?

NAT: Listen to him, more nostalgia! My poor schmeckle, talk about nostalgia! It comes up once a year, like Ground Hog Day. The last time I made love was July Tenth, Nineteen Seventy-One.

MIDGE: Was your wife still alive?

NAT: I certainly hope so.

MIDGE: No, I meant—

NAT: I know what you meant. With Ethel it wasn't always easy to tell. *(Smacks his forehead) Shame* on me! A good woman, a fine woman, was it *her* fault I would always be in love with Hannah Pearlman?

MIDGE: See, last time for me I was bein' unfaithful. Damn my fickle soul, I cheated on them all. Daisy, I was seventy-six, still had somethin' on the side; somethin' new.

NAT: Carter, this is the most courageous thing I ever heard about you.

MIDGE: No courage to it, it's a curse. "Don't do it, Midge; don't *do* it," I kept sayin' while I did it. *Damn* my cheatin' soul.

NAT: No, no, you were *right!* You dared and did, I yearned and regretted. I *envy* you. You were always what I have only recently become.

MIDGE: A dirty old man.

NAT: A *romanticist!* A man of hope! Listen to me, I was dead once so I know things—it's not the sex, it's the romance. It's all in the head. Now, finally, I know this. The schmeckle is out of business, but still the romance remains, the adventure. That's all there *ever* was. The body came along for the ride. Do you understand me, Carter?

MIDGE: I'm thinkin' about it . . .

NAT: Because, frankly, right now I'm in love with this girl here.

MIDGE: *(After a moment)* Well, fact is, so am I. I got to admit. *(Peers up at Laurie for a few seconds)* Son of a gun . . . First time I ever fell in love with a white woman.

NAT: The first? Why the first?

MIDGE: Worked out that way.

NAT: All the others were black? Only black women?

MIDGE: Listen, you ran with a wild, Commie crowd; where *I* come from you stuck with your own. Bein' a black man, I—

NAT: A what?

MIDGE: A black man. Y'see, in *my* day—

NAT: Wait. Stop. Excuse me . . . *(A beat; then Nat takes his bifocals out of his jacket pocket, puts them on, leans very close to Midge. He studies him for a few moments; then, quietly)* My God, you're right. You *are* a black man.

Silence for a moment. Then Nat bursts into laughter, pointing at Midge)

MIDGE: *(After a moment, catching on to the joke, a burst of laughter)* Sly devil, you sly ol' *devil* . . .

NAT: *(Laughing happily, pointing at Midge)* Hey, had ya goin', had ya *goin'* there for a minute, didn't I . . . ?

MIDGE: *(Claps his hands, delighted laughter building)* Had me goin', had me *goin'*, yeah . . . Lord, Lord . . .

NAT: *(Hitting his knees, roaring)* I love it, I love it, I love it—

(Fresh gales of stoned laughter; they rock on the bench)

MIDGE: Stop, stop, I'm gonna die . . .

NAT: I'm gonna drop dead right here . . . *(Suddenly stops laughing)* Wait a minute, Carter; is it *this* funny?

MIDGE: *(Stops laughing. Considers it. Bursts into laughter again)* Yes, it is. It is, definitely . . .

(They point at each other, laughing at each other's laughter, laughing now at the fact that they are laughing; they fall on each other, shaking with mirth, threatening to roll off the bench. Midge suddenly leans back on the bench and abruptly falls asleep, snoring loudly)

NAT: Carter, what are you doing? We're right in the middle . . . *(Midge keeps snoring)* How do you like that? One joint, look at this.

(Midge suddenly wakes up, rises to his feet, and, as if by request, bursts into song, singing "Alabamy Bound," gradually working in a small soft-shoe routine as he continues singing. Towards the end of the song Nat rises to his feet, inspired, joining in the soft-shoe, singing the rest of the song with Midge, the two finishing the song together with a grand, remembered, Vaudeville flourish. Laurie, who has been listening to Midge and Nat sing their song from her ledge on the bridge, far above them, smiles at them now, nods her approval, holds her hands up in a brief moment of applause, then returns to her sketching)

MIDGE: I think the woman's crazy about us.

NAT: Please, I knew it when she first showed up.

MIDGE: You got any more of that dope?

NAT: Now we're gonna do a Willy Howard routine. You think you were laughing *before*, wait'll you hear—

MIDGE: How about I do a Joe Turner song first, and *then* we do Willy Howard?

NAT: You just sang.

MIDGE: *(Sitting Nat on bench)* That was half an hour ago.

NAT: Really?

MIDGE: *(Looking up, announcing this for Laurie)* "So Long, Goodbye Blues," by Big Joe Turner, Boss of the Blues—

(Singing soulfully; a slow steady rhythm, snapping his fingers, performing for Laurie)
    "Well now, so long, goodbye baby
    Yeah, well, soon now I'm gonna be gone
    And that's why I'm sayin', baby—"

NAT: *(A burst of applause, rising)* That was exquisite. Now here's Willy Howard— *(Glancing up at Laurie, performing this for her)* O.K., Carter, I'm Willy Howard, you're the Straight Man. Whatever I say to you, you say to me, "I'm not Rappaport." You got that?

MIDGE: Yeah.

NAT: O.K., picture we just met.

MIDGE: O.K.

NAT: Hello, Rappaport!

MIDGE: I'm not Rappaport.

NAT: Hey, Rappaport, what happened to you? You used to be a tall, fat guy; now you're a short, skinny guy.

MIDGE: I'm not Rappaport.

NAT: You used to be a young fellah with a beard; now you're an old guy without a beard! What happened to you?

MIDGE: I'm not Rappaport.

NAT: What happened, Rappaport? You used to dress up nice; now you got old dirty clothes!

MIDGE: I'm not Rappaport.

NAT: And you changed your *name* too!

(A beat—then Nat bursts into laughter; even if he wasn't stoned, this routine would leave him helpless. Midge regards him solemnly, thinking it over—then suddenly gets it, joining Nat's laughter, pounding Nat's shoulder)

MIDGE: *(Through his laughter)* "And you changed your *name* too . . ." Lord, Lord . . . *(Shouting up at Laurie to make sure she got the punchline)* "And you changed your *name too!*"

DANFORTH'S VOICE: *(Shouting)* Right with you, Carter . . .

(Danforth enters on bridge, at left, jogging)

MIDGE: *(Still laughing)* Oh, shit; he's here . . .

DANFORTH: Right with you . . .

NAT: *(Laughing)* He's here! Good!

MIDGE: *(Trying to control his laughter)* He's here, gotta shape up, boy . . . *(Scurries to bench to get Nat's briefcase)*

NAT: *(Delighted)* Don't worry, we'll take care of him—

MIDGE: No, no, there's no *"we"*; there's no "we" here— *(Grips Nat's arm urgently, tries to stop himself from laughing)* You don't say *nothin'*, Mister, you don't open your *mouth* . . . *(A fresh burst of laughter)* You'll ruin me, boy; I'll be out on the street *tomorrow* . . .

(Danforth stops on bridge, winding down from his run, jogging in place, controlling his breaths, stretching himself against the bridge lamppost at right)

NAT: A piece of cake. The little I can see, the man is a wreck.

MIDGE: *(Still chuckling softly)* Please, *please*, baby . . . are you my friend?

NAT: Of course.

MIDGE: Then go over there, friend. *(Points to stone ledge, far left, at edge of lake)* Sit over there and don't open your mouth. Not a word.

NAT: *(After a moment)* You'll call me when you need me?

MIDGE: *(Hands Nat his briefcase)* Soon's I need you. Please, move it.

NAT: *(He has stopped chuckling)* O.K., O.K. . . . *(Reluctantly, he starts down left)* Remember, I'm ready.

MIDGE: I know that.

(Danforth, having completed his winding-down ritual on the bridge, starts down toward Midge at the bench, entering through the Tunnel Archway, mopping himself with a towel. Nat settles himself with some dignity on the far left ledge, some distance from them, crossing his legs, his briefcase and his cane at his side. Laurie has stretched out on the bridge ledge above, her eyes closed, a Walkman plugged into her ears, her shoulder-bag under her head)

DANFORTH: Carter, hi.

MIDGE: Hi.

DANFORTH: Don't think we've ever really been formally introduced. I'm Pete Danforth.

(They shake hands)

MIDGE: Hi, Pete. They call me "Midge."

DANFORTH: Hi, Midge. Glad we decided to meet here. Chance to stay outside; y'know, after my run. Truth is, I hate running. Being immortal takes too much time *(He chuckles)*

MIDGE: *(Sitting on bench)* "Midge" for midget. My third wife give me the name; near two and three-quarter inches taller'n me, so she called me "Midge." Name stuck with me fifty years.

DANFORTH: Tell ya one thing, it's good to be reminded of what a great park this is. Goddamn oasis in the middle of the jungle.

MIDGE: Next two wives was normal-sized women, so it didn't make much sense. Name stuck with me anyway.

DANFORTH: Luckily my teaching schedule gives me two free afternoons this semester. Chance to really use this park. It's been years. I teach Communication Arts over at the Manhattan Institute on Sixtieth. No air in the place. Dreary. Been thinking about holding one of my classes out here in the—

MIDGE: What kinda arts?

DANFORTH: Communication. Communication of all kinds. Personal, interpersonal, and public; pretty much the whole range of—

Judd Hirsch and Cleavon Little

Cleavon Little and Judd Hirsch

Ray Baker and Cleavon Little

Cheryl Giannini and Judd Hirsch

MIDGE: You teach talkin'.

DANFORTH: *(He smiles)* More or less; yes.

MIDGE: So you must know we at the end of the chit-chat section now. Right?

DANFORTH: Right, right . . . *(Sits next to Midge on bench, carefully folding his towel)* Funny thing, by the way, I really didn't know—that is, I wasn't aware until just a few days ago—that you actually worked in the building; that you were employed there.

MIDGE: Keep to myself. Do my job.

DANFORTH: Of course. I just wanted you to know that the problem we've got here had not come to my attention sooner simply because you, personally, had not come to my attention. Frankly, I've been living there three years and I've never run into you.

MIDGE: I'm mostly down in the boiler room; don't get a lot of drop-ins.

DANFORTH: Of course.

(Silence for a moment)

MIDGE: Keep movin', boy, you on a roll now.

DANFORTH: Yes, well, as you know, Three Twenty-One will be going Co-op in November. We'll be closing on that in November. We've got Brachman and Rader as our managing agent; I think they're doing an excel-

lent job. As President of the Tenants' Committee I'm
pretty much dependent, the whole Committee is really, on their advice; we've basically got to place our
faith in the recommendations of our Managing
Agency.

MIDGE: And they're recommendin' you dump me.

DANFORTH: Midge, we've got some real problems
about your remaining with the building staff.

MIDGE: Ain't that the same as dumpin' me?

DANFORTH: *(After a moment)* Midge, it's not for four
weeks, it's not till November, but, yes, we will have to
let you go. There are various benefits, Union Pension
Plan, six weeks severance pay; that's a check for six
weeks salary the day you leave, that's . . . Midge,
I'm sorry . . . *(Sadly; shaking his head)* God, I hate
this; I really hate this, Midge . . .

MIDGE: How 'bout *I* hate it first, then you get your turn.

DANFORTH: *(Quietly)* Midge, think about it, isn't this
the best thing for *every*body? The pressure on you,
tenants' complaints, trying to keep up. *(His hand on
Midge's arm)* Time, Midge—we're not dealing with
an evil Tenants' Committee or a heartless Managing
Agent—the only villain here is time. We're *all* fighting it. Jesus, man, have you seen me *run?* It's a joke. I
can't do what *I* did a few years ago either.

MIDGE: Hey, don't sweat it, son. See, Brachman and
Rader, all due respect, is full of shit. Fact is, you need

me. *(Leans back calmly)* Got an ol' Erie City boiler down there; heart of the buildin'. Things about that weird machine no livin' man knows, 'cept Midge Carter. Christmas. Take me till Christmas to train a new man how to handle that devil. *(Pats Danforth's knee)* You got it, have the new man set up for ya by Christmas.

DANFORTH: Midge, we're replacing the Erie City. We're installing a fully automatic Rockmill Five Hundred; it requires no maintenance. *(Silence for a moment; Midge does not respond)* You see, the Rockmill's just one of many steps in an extensive modernization plan; new electrical system, plumbing arteries, lobby renovation—

MIDGE: Well, *now* you're *really* gonna need me. Pipes, wires, you got forty years of temporary stuff in there, no blueprints gonna tell you where. Got it all in my head; know what's behind every wall, every stretch of tar. *(Clamps his hand on Danforth's shoulder)* O.K., here's the deal. My place in the basement, *I* stay on there free like I been, *you* get all my consultin' free. No *salary*, beauty deal for ya—

DANFORTH: Midge, to begin with, your unit in the basement is being placed on the co-op market as a garden apartment—

MIDGE: Don't you get it, baby? Blueprints, blueprints, I'm a walkin' treasure-map—

DANFORTH: Please understand, we've had a highly qualified team of building engineers doing a survey for months now—

MIDGE: *(Suddenly)* Hey, forget it.

DANFORTH: You see, they—

MIDGE: I said forget it. Ain't interested in the job no more. Don't *want* the job. Withdrawin' my offer. *(Turns away; opens his newspaper)*

DANFORTH: *(Moving closer)* Midge, listen to me . . .

MIDGE: Shit, all these years I been livin' in a garden apartment. Wished I knew sooner, woulda had a lot more parties.

DANFORTH: I have some news that I think will please you . . . *(His hand on Midge's arm)* Two of the older tenants on the Committee, Mrs. Carpenter, Mr. Lehman, have solved your relocation problem. Midge, there's an apartment for you at the Amsterdam. No waiting list for *you*, Mr. Lehman seems to know the right people. Caters especially to low-income senior adults and it's right here in the neighborhood you've grown used to—

MIDGE: Amsterdam's ninety percent foolish people. Ever been in the lobby there? Ever seen them sittin' there? Only way you can tell the live ones from the dead ones is how old their newspapers are.

DANFORTH: As I understood it from Mr. Lehman—

MIDGE: Amsterdam's the end of the line, boy.

DANFORTH: I'm sorry, I thought—

MIDGE: You ask Mr. Lehman *he* wants to go sit in that lobby; you ask Mrs. Carpenter *she* ready to leave the world. You tell 'em both "no thanks" from Midge, he's lookin' for a garden apartment.

DANFORTH: See, the problem is—

MIDGE: Problem is you givin' me bad guy news, tryin' to look like a good guy doin' it.

DANFORTH: *(After a moment)* You're right, Midge. You're right. You're dead right. *(Bows his head, genuinely upset)* I've handled this whole thing badly, stupidly, *stupidly.* I'm sorry, this whole thing . . . this is terrible . . .

MIDGE: *(Patting Danforth's hand)* Don't worry, Pete, you're gonna get through it.

DANFORTH: *(Rises, pacing in front of bench)* Damn it, I tell you what I *can* do—what I *will* do—I'm getting you *ten* weeks severance, Midge. *Forget* six, a check for ten weeks salary the day you go, I'm gonna hand it to you *personally.* And if the Committee doesn't agree, the hell with them; I'll shove it through, that's all. Least I can do. Ten weeks severance—how does that sound to ya?

MIDGE: Well, better than six, I guess . . . *(Nods thoughtfully)* Sounds better . . .

DANFORTH: *(Shaking Midge's hand with both of his)* That's a promise, Midge. Shove it down their throats if I have to. *(Moving briskly toward the stone steps at right to exit)* I'm sure we'll have no problem with—

NAT: Unacceptable. *(Calmly, rising from ledge at far left)* We find that unacceptable. *(Danforth stops, Nat moves slowly toward him)* Mr. Danforth . . . Mr. Danforth, I'll speak frankly, you're in a lot of trouble. *(Brisk handshake)* Ben Reissman; Reissman, Rothman, Rifkin and Grady. Forgive me for not announcing myself sooner, but I couldn't resist listening to you bury yourself. Our firm represents Mr. Carter, but, more to the point, we act as legal advisors to the HURTSFOE unit of Mr. Carter's union. HURTSFOE; I refer to the Human Rights Strike Force, a newly formed automatic-action unit who, I'm sorry to say, you're going to be hearing a lot from in the next few weeks. *(Sits next to Midge on bench, Danforth standing before them)* Personally, I find their methods too extreme; but I report and advise, that's all I can do. The ball is rolling here, Mr. Danforth.

MIDGE: Go away.

NAT: Mr. Carter keeps saying to us "go away"; we were arguing this very point as you ran by earlier. But, of course, as he knows, we are an automatic function of his union for the protection of all members. I have no choice.

MIDGE: *(Grips Nat's arm)* Man wants to give me ten weeks severance—

NAT: A joke. The fellow is obviously a jokester.

DANFORTH: Mr. Reissman—

NAT: Speak to me.

DANFORTH: I'm not sure that I understand the—

NAT: Of course not. How could you? *(Crosses his legs, continuing calmly)* I will educate you. The situation is simple, I will make it simpler. We don't accept ten weeks severance, we don't accept twenty. What we accept is that Mr. Carter be retained in the capacity of advisor during your reconstruction period, which I assume will take a year, maybe two. At this point, we'll talk further.

MIDGE: *(To Danforth)* I don't know him; I don't *know* this man.

NAT: Quite so; Mr. Carter is more familiar with Rifkin and Grady, the gentler gentlemen in our firm. It was thought best to send "The Cobra" in on this one. An affectionate term for me at the office.

DANFORTH: *(Sharply)* Look, Reissman—

NAT: Speak to me.

DANFORTH: *(Steps toward him, firmly)* I don't know what your game is, fellah, and I don't know your organization; but I *do* know Local Thirty-Two of the Service Employees Union—

NAT: And do *they* know you're planning to fire Mr. Carter?

DANFORTH: Not yet, but we—

NAT: And do *you* know that there's no mandatory retirement age in Mr. Carter's union? And do *you* know, further, that this means Carter has the right to call an arbitration hearing where he can defend his competence? And that you will have to get a minimum of four tenants to *testify* against him? Oh, that will be interesting. *Find* them. I want to *see* this, Danforth. Four tenants who want to be responsible—*publicly* responsible—for putting this old man out of his home and profession of forty-two years. *(His hand on Midge's shoulder)* A man who was named "Super of the Year" by the New York *Post* in Nineteen Sixty-Eight; a man who fought in World War Two, a man who served with the now legendary Black Battalion of Bastogne at the Battle of the Bulge. The clippings will be Xeroxed and circulated, the worms you find to testify will be informed. *(Rises from bench, pointing cane at Danforth) And—and* are you aware that for as long as you insist on pursuing this matter, for as long as this hearing lasts—and I promise you we will make it a *long* one—you can *make* no contract with Local Thirty-Two? That without a union contract you can *have* no co-op sale, no building corporation? Time, my friend, time will be *your* villain now. My firm will go *beyond* this hearing if justice fails us there. I'm talking *months,* cookie; I'm talking litigation, appeals, the full weight and guile of Rothman, Rifkin, Grady, and The Cobra. *(He lowers his cane to his side, moves slowly toward Danforth; quietly)* Sir,

I urge you to consider, win or lose, the massive and draining legal fees you will incur in pursuing this. I urge you to compare this time, cost, and embarrassment to the tiny sum it will take to keep Mr. Carter on salary. I urge you for *all* our sakes.

(Danforth stands there in silence for a few moments, clearly confused. Midge has remained on the bench, listening with fascination)

DANFORTH: Reissman . . .

NAT: Speak to me.

DANFORTH: I'm, frankly, a little thrown by this. I . . . I mean, you're asking me to just accept—

NAT: Accept or don't accept; I'm obligated to report this to HURTSFOE immediately.

DANFORTH: I knew about the right to arbitration— Midge, I just didn't think you'd really want—

NAT: He wants. Meanwhile HURTSFOE goes after you tomorrow anyway. They'll make an example of you, you're perfect for them—

DANFORTH: But what have I—?

NAT: Idiot, you've hit every human rights nerve there is. I'm talking old, I'm talking black, I'm talking racial imbalance—

DANFORTH: Racial *imbalance?* The man was walking into *walls.* For God's sake, the man's an easy *eighty.*

NAT: There's nothing, I promise you, easy about eighty. Damn it, why am I even bothering to *warn* you? *(Picks up his briefcase)* Tomorrow you'll see it all. Time to let HURTSFOE out of its cage— *(Turns sharply, starts walking toward stone steps at right, to exit)*

DANFORTH: *(Moves toward him, angrily)* Now look, Reissman, I find it hard to believe that I would be held personally responsible for—

NAT: *(Starting briskly up steps)* You'll believe it tomorrow when they picket in front of your school. What was the name of that place, the Manhattan Institute? They'll believe it too. And then the demonstrations in front of your apartment building— *(Stops halfway up steps, pointing cane down at Danforth)* The name Danforth will start to *mean* something—you'll become an *adjective*, my friend, a symbol, a new word for the persecution of the old and disabled, the black and the blind!

DANFORTH: Wait a minute—

NAT: *Do* it, Danforth, *fire* him, it's your one shot at immortality! *Do* it . . . *(Midge holds his hand up in alarm)* Yes, Carter, forgive me, I *want* it to happen . . . I want to see HURTSFOE in action again . . . *(Tenderly, looking away)* Those crazy wildcats, it's hard not to love them. Those mad, inspired men. I want to hear the old words, alive again and pure . . . "Strike for a humane existence" . . . "Strike for universal justice"— *(His cane in the air, shouting)* Strike, strike—

DANFORTH: *(Shouting)* Hold it! Wait a minute! This
. . . this whole goddamn mess has gotten out of hand
. . . *(Continuing firmly)* Reissman, believe me, this
was never my own, personal thing; I represent a
Committee, the joint wishes of a—

NAT: I'm sorry, the spotlight falls on you because it
must. Because you are so extraordinarily ordinary,
because there are so many of you now. *(Starts down
steps toward him)* You collect old furniture, old cars,
old pictures, everything old but old people. Bad sou-
venirs, they talk too much. Even quiet, they tell you
too much; they look like the future and you don't
want to know. Who *are* these people, these oldies,
this strange race? They're not my type, put them
with their own *kind,* a building, a town, *put* them
someplace. *(Leans toward him)* You idiots, don't you
know? One day you *too* will join this weird tribe. Yes,
Mr. Chairman, you *will* get old; I hate to break the
news. And if you're frightened now, you'll be terrified then. The problem's *not* that life is short but that
it's very long; so you better have a policy. Here we
are. Look at us. We're the coming attractions. And as
long as you're afraid of *it,* you'll be afraid of *us,* you
will want to hide us or make us hide from you. You're
dangerous. *(Grips his arm urgently)* You foolish bas-
tards, don't you under*stand?* The old people, they're
the *survivors,* they *know* something, they haven't just
stayed late to ruin your party. The very old, they are
miracles like the just-born; close to the end is pre-
cious like close to the beginning. What you'd like is
for Carter to be nice and cute and quiet and go away.
But he won't. I won't let him. Tell him he's slow or

stupid—O.K.—but you tell him that he is unnecessary, and that is a sin, that is a sin against life, that is abortion at the other end. *(Silence; Nat studies him for a moment)* HURTSFOE waits. The arena is booked, the lions are hungry . . .

DANFORTH: *(Quietly, earnestly)* Ben, I'm glad you shared these thoughts with me. I'd never really—

NAT: I'm through communicating with you, I'm communicating with Carter now. *(Sits next to Midge on bench)* Carter, what shall we do with him? I leave it to you.

MIDGE: I think . . . I think we should give him a break.

DANFORTH: Ben, I'm sure that I can persuade the members of the Committee to reevaluate Midge's—

NAT: Carter, what are you *saying?* What happens to the Cause? Are you saying you just want to keep your job and forget about the Cause?

MIDGE: Frankly, yes; that's what I'm sayin'. Forget the Cause, keep the job.

DANFORTH: *(Perches opposite them on small bench)* I think it's essential that we avoid any extreme—

NAT: Carter, are you asking The Cobra *not* to strike?

MIDGE: Don't want that Cobra to strike, no.

DANFORTH: Next Committee meeting's in two weeks. I'll explain the—

NAT: Mr. Danforth, my client has instructed me to save your ass. Quickly, the bomb is ticking . . . *(Danforth leans toward him intently)* Two weeks is too late. Tonight. Jog home to your phone, call the members of your committee. Don't persuade, don't explain; announce. Tell them there's a job for Carter. Guide. Counselor. How about Superintendent Emeritus? Has a nice sound to it. Meanwhile, speak to *no* one—the union, your managing agent, *no* one. HURTSFOE gets wind of this, we're *all* in trouble. *(Hands him business card from briefcase)* When you're finished with the Committee, call here. Before ten tomorrow if you want to stop HURTSFOE. Speak only to the lady on the card, Mrs. Clara Gelber; tell her to reach a man called "Pop"—he's one of HURTSFOE's top people—tell her to inform him that the Carter matter has been resolved, this "Pop" fellow will take it from there.

DANFORTH: *(Reading from card)* "Park East Real Estate Agency . . ."

NAT: HURTSFOE's advisory group; smart people, good hearts, they negotiate with management. *(Hands him another card)* Here; if there's trouble tonight, call me— *(They both rise)* That's my club on Eighty-Sixth, ask for Dr. Engels, he'll contact me. *(Pats Danforth's cheek)* Goodbye and good luck.

(Danforth moves briskly toward the stone steps; stops, turns to them)

DANFORTH: *(Quietly)* Midge . . . Ben . . . I want you to know that this has been a very important conversation for me, for *many* reasons . . . a lot of primary thoughts . . .

NAT: I think it's been an important conversation for all of us. Goodbye.

DANFORTH: An important exchange of ideas, a . . . a sudden awareness of certain generational values that I—

NAT: I warn you, one more word and there'll be a citizen's arrest for crimes against the language.

DANFORTH: *(He smiles, shakes his head)* Fact is, certain areas, I *do* have trouble talking . . .

NAT: Also leaving. Go now, the phone! *(Danforth races briskly up the steps)* Quickly. Let me see those sneakers flash!

(Danforth exits. Nat turns triumphantly toward Midge, his cane held high in the air like a sword of victory)

MIDGE: *(He slumps forward on the bench)* Never; we ain't never gettin' away with this . . .

NAT: *(To himself, smiling)* Truth is, I always *did* want to be a lawyer . . . but years ago there were so many choices . . .

MIDGE: Black Battalion of *Bastogne?* . . . We ain't never gettin' away with this . . . Gonna catch *on* to us, only a matter of *time* now; find out you ain't no lawyer, find out there ain't no HURTSFOE—

NAT: You're better off than you were twenty minutes ago, right? You still have your job, don't you? A week, a month, by then I'll have a *better* idea, *another* plan. What's wrong with you? Why aren't you awed by this triumph? Why aren't you embracing me?

MIDGE: *(Rising, angrily)* Was playin' that boy just *right* 'fore you opened your mouth. Had him goin' for extra severance—catches on now, I lose it *all*. What I do to deserve you? What I *do*, Reissman—

NAT: I'm not Reissman. Reissman is the name of my pickpocket surgeon.

MIDGE: O.K., *Schwartz*man, you're Sam Schwartz-man—

NAT: Not him either.

MIDGE: Then who the hell *are* you, Mister? Shit, if you ain't Hernando and you ain't Schwartzman, and you ain't Rappaport, then—

NAT: *(Softly, looking away)* Just now I was Ben Gold. I was Ben for a while . . . You use who you need for the occasion. An occasion arises and one chooses a suitable person to—

(During these last few lines Gilley has stepped forward from the shadows on the bridge above, at left, near the ledge where Laurie has drifted off to sleep—a sudden

*sense of his presence has awakened her; frightened, she
has swept up her bag and art supplies, raced across the
bridge and exited at right. Gilley is an Irish kid, about
sixteen; an impassive, experienced, and almost unread-
able face. The faded color of his jeans and jean jacket
and his careful, economical movements make him in-
conspicuous and, in a sense, part of the park; for all we
know he may have been standing there in the shadows
for an hour. He has a constant awareness of everything
around him, the precision of a pro and the instincts of a
street creature. We hear the distant sound of the Carousel Band-Organ playing "Queen City March," the last
melody of the fading day. During the last fifteen minutes or so the pretty colors of the autumn afternoon
have gradually given way to the dark shadows of early
evening, the faint chatter of crickets and the lonely
lights of the two lampposts on the bridge, reminding us
of the isolated and near-empty section of the park we
are in. Gilley stands quite still now on the bridge, a
silhouette beneath the lamplight, looking off at what
must be the other benches along the lakeside, studying
the few remaining people on them and their posses-
sions, considering the possibilities.*

*Nat has suddenly interrupted his last speech to look up
at the Bridge)*

NAT: Who's that? There's no glow, the girl is gone.

*(Midge knows the all too familiar figure on the bridge
and that it is the appointed "collection" time; he turns
away, trying to look unconcerned)*

MIDGE: Nobody. That's nobody.

NAT: That's *him*, right? The punk.

MIDGE: Ain't *the* punk, just some punk.

NAT: That's our punk, isn't it?

MIDGE: Not *our* punk, not *our* punk; just *my* punk.

NAT: Excuse me, I have something to discuss with him—

(He starts toward the Bridge—Midge grabs both of Nat's arms and quite forcefully pulls him back—Gilley starts slowly, casually down the back stairs to the Tunnel, toward Midge and Nat)

MIDGE: *(A strong grip on Nat, whispering urgently)* Now you listen here to *me*, No-Name. This kid, you run your mouth on *him* he finish you, then finish me sure. Sit down— *(Shoves Nat down on bench, sits next to him)* These kids is crazy; beat up old folks for *exercise*, boy. Sass this kid, he stomp us *good*— *(Pointing to the offstage benches)* and these folks here, while he's doin' it they gonna keep *score*, gonna watch like it's happenin' on the TV.

(Gilley appears in the darkened Tunnel, some distance behind them. He remains quite still, deep in the Tunnel, waiting)

MIDGE: Toll on this bridge is three dollars and that bridge gonna take me home. *(Rises, taking his newspaper)* Call it a *day*, boy. See you sometime.

(Midge starts into the Tunnel toward the waiting Gilley. Silence for a moment)

GILLEY: *(Flatly)* Who's this?

MIDGE: Friend of mine.

GILLEY: Where's he live?

MIDGE: Dunno. Hangs out here; he—

GILLEY: *(Moves down behind Nat's bench, leans toward him; quietly)* Where you live?

NAT: First I'll tell you where I work. I work at the Nineteenth Precinct— *(Turns, holds out his hand)* Danforth; Captain Pete Danforth, Special Projects, I—

GILLEY: *(Takes his hand; not shaking it, just holding it tightly)* Where you live?

NAT: Not far, but I'm—

GILLEY: Walk you home, y'know.

NAT: That won't be necessary, it's—

GILLEY: Cost you three.

NAT: Listen, son, I don't need—

GILLEY: Cost you four. Just went up to four, y'know. *(To both)* Saw this lady this morning. Dog-walker, y'know. Five, six dogs at a time. Give me an idea. Walk you both home. Terrific idea, huh? *(To Nat)* Terrific idea, right? *(Silence for a moment. Gilley tightens his grip on Nat's hand. Nat nods in agreement. Gilley lets go of his hand; pats Nat gently on the head)* Right. Walk you both; four each.

MIDGE: But our deal was—

GILLEY: Four.

MIDGE: O.K.

GILLEY: Right. *(Starts into Tunnel)* O.K., boys; everybody walkin'; convoy movin' out. *(Midge walks dutifully behind Gilley. Nat remains seated. A moment; Gilley moves slowly back to Nat's bench, stands behind him)* Hey, that's everybody, right? *(Silence for a moment. Nat hesitates; then picks up his briefcase and slowly, obediently rises, his head bowed. Gilley nods his approval, turns, starts walking into the Tunnel; Midge following)* O.K.; nice and slow; movin' out, headin' home, boys . . .

(Nat remains standing at the bench. This immobility is not a conscious decision on Nat's part; he just finds himself, quite simply, unable to move)

MIDGE: *(Stops, turns to Nat; a frightened whisper)* Come on, *please*, move . . . *move*, Mister . . .

(Gilley stops in the Tunnel, aware that he is not being followed. He turns to Nat; starts quickly to the bench, shoving Midge out of his way as he moves toward Nat.

Nat holds his hand up urgently, Gilley stops just in front of him)

NAT: *(Quickly)* Take it easy, I don't fight with Irish kids. I know the same thing now that I knew sixty-five years ago: don't fight with an Irish kid. *(Points to him)* How did I know Irish? I hear; I know all the sounds. But better, I know the feelings. This is because sixty-five years ago I was you. Irish kids, Italian, Russian, we *all* stole. Then, like now, the city lives by Darwin; this means everybody's on somebody's menu—*(Passionately, moving closer to him)* Trouble is, you got the wrong supper here. Me and Midge, you're noshing on your own. We live in the streets and the parks, we're dead if we stay home; just like you, Gilley. You're angry. You should be. So am I. But the trouble's at the top, like always—the Big Boys, the Fat Cats, the String-Pullers, the *top*—we're down here with you, kid. You, me, Midge, we have the same enemy, we have to stick together or we're finished. It's the only chance we got.

(Silence for a moment)

GILLEY: Five. Went up to five. Y'mouth just cost ya a dollar. *(Nat does not respond. Gilley holds out his hand)* O.K., that's five; in advance, y'know.

NAT: *(Softly)* No. I can't do that. I won't do that. Gilley, please understand; we mustn't do this. *(Touching his jacket pocket)* I have twenty-two dollars; I would share it with you, gladly share. But not like *this;* not us . . .

GILLEY: Great. Gimme the twenty-two. *(Shaking his head)* Y'mouth, I'm tellin' ya. It's costin', y'know.

NAT: *(Quietly, sadly)* I'm . . . I'm very disappointed . . .

MIDGE: *(Whispering)* Give it to him.

NAT: I can't do that, kid; not *all;* that's unreasonable. *(Gilley reaches for Nat's pocket, Nat shoves his hand sharply away)* I have limited funds. I can't do that.

GILLEY: *(Calmly takes hunting knife in fancy leather sheath from his belt; unsheathes the knife, holding it down at his side)* Ask you once more.

MIDGE: *(From Tunnel, trembling)* Please, *give* it to him, Mister . . . please . . .

NAT: Gilley, this is a mistake. Don't do this. *(Gilley glances quickly about the area to see if he is being observed, then holds up his knife; a demonstration)* No, no knives, not for us. Not between us. We're together—

(Nat makes a sharp underhand move with his cane, hitting Gilley's wrist; Gilley drops the knife, holding his wrist in pain and surprise; Gilley looks at Midge as though to ask for aid with a misbehaving child, then kneels down quickly to pick up his knife. Nat, more in fear and frustration than courage, raises his cane in the air with both hands, shouting—an angry, guttural, old battle cry—and strikes a sharp blow on the back of the kneeling Gilley. Gilley cries out in pain, rising, out-

raged, leaving his knife, slapping the cane out of Nat's hand—Nat steps back, helpless now; Gilley grabs him by both shoulders and swings him around fiercely, flinging him backward with a powerful throw, Nat falling back against the stone ledge at the edge of the lake, hitting the ledge sharply and then rolling off onto the path where he lies quite still, face down, away from us. Gilley glances about, grabs up the wallet from Nat's coat, then moves quickly toward the Tunnel, shouting over his shoulder at Midge)

GILLEY: Tell your friend the rules! You better tell your friend the rules, man—

(Gilley stops—looks back at the very still form of Nat—then races quickly off into the darkened Tunnel, forgetting his knife, disappearing into the shadows of the park.

Midge moves down toward Nat as quickly as possible, kneels next to him)

MIDGE: *(Quietly)* Hey . . . hey, Mister . . . ? *(Silence. He touches Nat, gently)* Come on now, wake up . . . wake up . . .

(Nat remains quite still. Silence again. Midge rises to his feet, shouting out at the lake)

MIDGE: Help! . . . Over here! . . . *(No response. Midge looks out across the lake, a near-blind old man staring into the darkness around him)* Look what we got here! . . .

(Silence again; only the sound of the early evening crickets. The park grows darker, Midge's face barely visible now in the lamplight as . . .

THE CURTAIN FALLS)

Act Two

SCENE: *The same; three in the afternoon, the next day. Before the curtain rises we hear the Carousel Band-Organ playing "We All Scream For Ice Cream."*

AT RISE: *Midge is alone on the path; he is seated at the far left end of the center bench, his newspaper unopened on his lap, looking straight ahead, unable to relax in the pleasant sunlight that shines on the bench. The Carousel Music continues distantly now; the melody drifts in and out with the gentle autumn breeze. Laurie is in her usual position on the bridge, far above Midge, sketching dreamily. Midge continues looking solemnly out at the lake. A full minute passes.*

We begin to hear Nat's voice, off left, singing "Ain't We Got Fun," approaching slowly. Midge looks left, then immediately opens his newspaper, holds it up to his bifocals, "reading." Nat enters Up Left, moving slowly down the path within an aluminum walker. The walker is a three-sided, four-legged device with three metal braces holding the sides together; his briefcase and cane are hooked over two of the braces; there is a three-inch gauze bandage above his right eye. Although Nat moves very slowly he manages to incorporate the walker into his natural elegance, using the walker rhythmically rather than haltingly, a steady ambulatory tempo to the bouncy beat of his song, as he approaches the bench. Midge is turned away with his newspaper, ignoring him completely.

Nat continues toward the bench, singing the song with great gusto, pausing momentarily to tap his walker on the path for rhythmic emphasis, then continuing to the bench, parking the walker next to it as he finishes the last line of the song. Nat sits carefully on the bench. Midge continues to read his newspapers making no acknowledgement of Nat's arrival.

NAT: *(Rubbing his hands together)* Well, that punk, we got him on the run now. *(He leans back comfortably)* Yessir, got him where we want him now. *(Jabbing the air)* Boom, on the arm I got him; boom on the back. Boom, boom, boom—

MIDGE: *(Not looking up from paper)* Tell me somethin', Rocky; you plannin' to sit here on this bench? 'Cause if you *are*, I got to move to another spot.

NAT: I'm sure you were about to inquire about my health. *(Taps his hip)* Only a slight sprain, no breaks, no dislocations. I am an expert at falling down. I have a gift for it. The emergency room at Roosevelt was twenty dollars. Not a bad price for keeping the bandit at bay.

MIDGE: *(Folding newspaper)* *You* movin' or am *I* movin'? Answer me.

NAT: I guarantee he will not return today. He wants the easy money, he doesn't want trouble—

MIDGE: *(Puts on his hat)* O.K., leavin' now . . .

NAT: And if by some odd chance he *does* return, I feel we were close to an understanding. We must realize, you and I, that this boy is caught like us in the same dog eat dog trap—

MIDGE: *(He rises)* Goodbye; gonna leave you two dogs to talk it over. Movin' on now.

NAT: Wait, Carter—

MIDGE: *(Leans close to him)* Can't see your face too good; what I *can* see got cemetery written all over it. So long for *good,* baby.

NAT: Sir, a friendship like ours is a rare—

MIDGE: Ain't no friendship. Never *was* no friendship. Don't even know your goddamn *name.*

NAT: Yesterday you helped a fallen comrade—

MIDGE: You was out *cold,* Mister. Waited for the ambulance to come, done my duty same's I would for *any* lame dog. Said to myself, that ain't gonna be *me* lyin' there. *(Takes Gilley's leather sheathed hunting knife from pocket)* See this item here? Kid run off without his weapon, see. He comin' back for it today sure. I come here to give it back to him, stay on that boy's *good* side. *(Starts down path toward stone ledge at far left)* O.K., waitin' over here so he sees you and me is no longer *associated;* which we *ain't,* got that? He comes, don't want you *talkin'* to me, *lookin'* at me, contactin' me any way whatever.

NAT: So; the Cossack leaves his sword and you return it.

MIDGE: You bet. *(Settles down on ledge)*

NAT: *(Leans toward him)* You have had a taste of revolution and will not be able to return to subjection, to living in an occupied country!

MIDGE: Watch me.

(Midge closes his eyes, puts his huge handkerchief over his face, curls up on ledge.

Clara enters on the stone steps at right; attractive, early forties, stylishly bohemian clothes; she is walking quickly, purposefully down the steps toward Nat's bench. Nat rises, using the bench for support, unaware of the approaching Clara, pointing his cane at Midge)

NAT: No, *no*, you must not pay this punk for your existence, to live in your own land!

MIDGE: *(From under the handkerchief)* Nap time now. You're talkin' to nobody.

NAT: Exactly! No one! Surrender to the oppressors and you are no one! *(Midge begins to snore quietly)* Sure, sleep! Sleep then, like any bum in the park—

CLARA: *(Stopping on steps)* Excuse me . . .

NAT: *(Still to Midge)* A *napper* . . .

CLARA: Excuse me, I hate to interrupt you when you're driving somebody crazy . . .

NAT: A napper and a groveler! Why did I waste my time?!

CLARA: *(Seeing the walker, the bandage; concerned, frightened, moving toward bench)* God, what happened? . . . Are you all right?

NAT: Everything's fine; don't worry, don't worry . . .

CLARA: Stitches this time?

NAT: A scratch.

CLARA: Your hip?

NAT: A sprain, a sprain . . .

CLARA: Dad, what happened? Why didn't you *call* me? Another fight, right? You got into another fight, didn't you?

NAT: *(Sits on small bench)* What fights? I don't fight.

CLARA: How about four weeks ago? How about attacking that poor butcher at Gristede's? What was that?

NAT: I didn't attack the butcher. I attacked the meat. That was because of the prices.

CLARA: He said you shoved all the meat off his display counter with your cane—

NAT: It was a demonstration—there were thirty people in the store, I was trying to rally them, the meat shoving was an illustration—

CLARA: The meat hit the butcher and you threw out your hip. Also the chances of starting a commune on Seventy-Second and Broadway are very slim. What happened this time, Dad?

NAT: Well, a young boy—confused, disadvantaged, a victim of society—

CLARA: A mugger. *(She nods)* You fought with a mugger. *(Pacing anxiously behind center bench)* Of course, of course, it was the next step; my God . . .

NAT: We were talking; we reached an impasse—

CLARA: That's it. No more. I can't let this happen anymore. I let it go, I've been irresponsible. You have to be watched. I'm not letting you out of my sight, Dad.

NAT: Stop this, you're frightening me . . .

CLARA: Oh, *I'm* frightening *you*, huh? I live in terror—the phone will ring, the police, the hospital. My God. It was quiet for a month, but I should have known. This guy Danforth calls this morning and I know you're on the loose again—

NAT: Ah, good, he called—

CLARA: Oh, he *called* all right— *(Takes out message; reads)* "Tell HURTSFOE that the Carter matter is settled; I reached the Committee; Reissman said to call." . . . Jesus, *HURTSFOE* again; HURTSFOE's on the march again. I take it you're Reissman.

NAT: That was yesterday—

CLARA: And tomorrow who? And tomorrow *what?* I came to tell you it's the last *time!* No more calls—

NAT: You *covered*, didn't you?

CLARA: Yes, yes. Once again, once again. Christ, in one year I've been the headquarters for the Eighth Congressional District, CBS News, the Institute for Freudian Studies, and the United Consumers Protection Agency . . .

NAT: *(Fondly)* Ah, yes, *UCPA* . . .

CLARA: *(Sighs, nodding)* UCPA, UCPA . . . Look, Dad—

NAT: What's *happened* to you? My own daughter has forgotten what a principle is!

CLARA: *What* principle? There's no *principle* here. It's fraud. Personal, daily fraud. A one-man reign of terror and I'm the one who gets terrorized. Never knowing who the hell I'm supposed to be everytime some poor sucker calls my office. A *principle?* You mean when that panic-stricken manager of the Fine Arts Theatre called thinking there was going to be a Congressional Investigation because he showed German movies? I *still* don't understand how you convinced him you were a congressman—

NAT: What, you never saw an elder statesman before?

CLARA: But there's no such *thing* as a Floating Congressional District—

NAT: It's *because* he didn't know that he deserved it! That and showing movies by ex-Nazis. These people think that nobody *notices,* Clara—

CLARA: No *more!* It's over! Today was my last cover, that's what I came to tell you. Little did I know you were also back in combat again. *(Sits on center bench, opposite him)* Searched this damn park for two hours —*(Pointing up right)* What happened? You're not giving speeches at the Bethesda Fountain anymore?

NAT: Why should I? So you can find me there? shut me up, embarrass me?

CLARA: It's *me,* huh? It's me who embarrasses *you*—

NAT: Exactly; hushing me like I was a babbling child, a—

CLARA: Embarrassment, let's talk about embarrassment, O.K.? Three weeks ago I come back to my office after lunch, they tell me my Parole Officer was looking for me.

NAT: *(Bangs his cane on the ground)* Necessary retaliation! It was important that you see what it's like to be pursued, watched, guarded . . . *(Turns to her, quietly)* You *do* frighten me, Mrs. Gelber. You do frighten me, you know. I'm afraid of what you'll do out of what you think is love. Coming to the Fountain once a week—it's not stopping me from talking; that's not so bad. It's the test questions.

CLARA: I don't—

NAT: The test questions to see if I'm too old. *(Taps his head)* Checking on the arteries. "Do you remember what you did yesterday, Dad?" "Tell me what you had for lunch today, Dad?" One wrong answer you'll wrap me in a deck chair and mail me to Florida; *two* mistakes you'll put me in a home for the forgettable. I know this. My greatest fear is that someday soon I will wake up silly, that time will take my brain and you will take me. That you will put me in a place, a home —or worse, *your* house. Siberia in Great Neck. Very little frightens me, as you know; just that. Only what you will do.

CLARA: Dad . . .

NAT: I don't answer the door when you come. That's why. I watch through the hole in the door and wait for you to go away. That's why I moved from the Fountain, Clara. And why next week you won't find me *here* either.

CLARA: *(After a moment)* You don't understand; I . . . I care . . . Someone has to watch out for you. Jack doesn't care, or Ben or Carole. They don't even speak to you anymore.

NAT: Good; God bless them; lovely children. Lovely, distant children.

CLARA: This isn't fair, Dad; I don't deserve this . . .

NAT: Dad. Who is this "Dad" you refer to? When did *that* start? I'm a "Pop," a Pop or a Papa, like I always was. You say "Dad" I keep looking around for a gentleman with a pipe.

CLARA: O.K., why don't I just call you "Dr. Engels" then? *(Silence for a moment. Nat turns to her)* Did you really think you fooled me? Dr. Engels the therapist? Dr. Fred Engels from the Socialists' Club? Really now.

NAT: But why did you keep writing all those letters to him—?

CLARA: Normal conversation with you is hopeless. Seemed like the best way to reach you. I sent "Dr. Engels" twelve letters in two months, I said everything I felt.

NAT: Smart. Smart girl. Well, at least you're still smart . . . even though the passions are gone, even though the ideals have evaporated . . .

CLARA: Stop . . .

NAT: I remember when you believed that the world did *not* belong to the highest bidder . . .

CLARA: The old song, stop . . .

NAT: This, of course, was before you went into Park East Real Estate, before you gave up Marx and Lenin for Bergdorf and Goodman . . .

CLARA: Jesus, at least get a new set of words—

NAT: Look at you! Look what you've become! Queen of the Condominiums, peasant skirts for two hundred dollars, betrayer of your namesake—

CLARA: Goddamn *name*—

NAT: Clara Lemlich, who stood for something—

CLARA: You *gave* me the name; I had no *choice*—

NAT: Clara Lemlich, who stood for something and stood up for it . . .

CLARA: *(Leans back on bench)* Ah, you're rolling now . . .

NAT: Cooper Union; November, Nineteen-Nine . . .

CLARA: You're only eight . . .

NAT: *(Looking away)* I'm only eight, the Shirtwaist Makers are there, thousands of them . . .

CLARA: *(Whispering)* You're standing in back with your father . . .

NAT: I'm standing in the back with my father; he holds me up so I can see. A meeting has been called to protest conditions. Gompers speaks, and Mary Drier, Panken, and Myer London. All speak well and with passion, but none with the courage to call a general strike. All speak of the bosses who value property above life and profits above people, but all speak with caution . . .

CLARA: *(Whispering)* Until suddenly . . .

NAT: Until suddenly from the back of the hall, just near us, rises a skinny girl, a teenager; she runs up onto the platform, this little girl, she runs up unafraid among the great ones; she shouts in Yiddish to the thousands, this girl, with the power of inspiration . . . this girl is Clara Lemlich. "I am a working girl, one of those striking against intolerable conditions. I am *tired* of listening to speakers! I offer a resolution that a general strike be called—*now!*" *(Softly)* A moment of shock . . . and then the crowd screams, feet pound the floor! The chairman, Feigenbaum, calls for a second; the thousands cry "Second!" in one voice. Feigenbaum trembles, shouts to the hall, "Do you mean this in good faith? Will you take the Jewish oath?" Three thousand hands are raised—my father is holding me up; his hands are not free. "Raise your hand, boy, raise your hand for us and I will say the oath"— My hand goes up; I feel his heart beating at my back as my father with the thousands chants the solemn oath: "If I turn traitor to the cause I now pledge, may this hand wither from the arm I raise!" Again there is silence in the hall . . .

CLARA: *(Softly; caught up in the story again, as always)* And then Feigenbaum shouts . . .

NAT: And Feigenbaum shouts—*(He raises his fist in the air)* a general strike has been called! *(A moment; then he lowers his fist)* Thirty-two years later, December, Forty-One, Roosevelt vows vengeance upon the Fascists, and the next day *you* are born with a powerful scream at Kings County Hospital—I say to your mother, "Ethel, sounds to me like Clara Lemlich." This is the name . . .

CLARA AND NAT: *(Together)* And this is the passion you were born with . . .

CLARA: *Finis.*

NAT: *(Turns to her)* And only forty-one years later you have turned into my own, personal K.G.B.

CLARA: Go to hell.

NAT: I can't; you'll follow me.

(She turns to him, sharply)

CLARA: Clara, Clara—it's not a name, it's a curse. The Cause, the goddamn *Cause*—everybody else gets a two-wheeler when they're ten, I got *Das Kapital* in paperback. Sundays you sent me out for bagels and lox and the weekend *Daily Worker;* I hide it in the bag so half of Flatbush Avenue doesn't point at me. Fights at school, kids avoiding me, daughter of the Reds. My friend Sally—my *only* friend—we're down in the street on a Saturday morning; she tells me she believes in God. I'm confused, I run upstairs to the Central Committee; "Pop, Sally Marcus says she believes in God. What should I tell her?" "Tell her she'll get over it," you say. I tell her, she tells her mother, and the next day I got *no*body on the block to play with; *alone* again, *alone*—

NAT: *(Leans toward her)* Unfair! This isn't *fair.* Later you believed in your *own* things and I loved you for it. You gave up on the Party, I respected you. The Civil Rights, the Anti-war; you marched, you demonstrated, you *spoke*—that was *you,* nobody *made* you, you loved it—

CLARA: I *did* love it—

NAT: You *changed*—

CLARA: No, I just noticed that the world didn't.

NAT: Ah, first it was me, then it was the world. It's nice to know who to blame. Ten *years,* what have you done?

CLARA: What have I *done?* I got married and had two children and lived a life. I got smarter and fought in battles I figured I could win. That's what I've done.

NAT: Lovely. And now, at last, everybody on the block plays with you, don't they? Yes, all the kids play with you now. You married Ricky the smiling Radiologist; he overcharged his way into a house in Great Neck where your children, as far as I can see, believe firmly in Cable Television. They'll fight to the death for it! And all the kids play with *them* too. It's the new utopia: everybody plays with everybody! My enemies, I keep up! My enemies, I don't forget; I cherish them like my friends, so I know what to *do*—

CLARA: And what's that? What the hell do you do? Lead raids on lambchops at Gristede's? Oh, God, it's all so easy for you, I almost envy you. You always know what side to be on because you fight old wars; old, old wars . . . *(At bench, leaning toward him)* The battle is *over*, Comrade; didn't you notice? Nothing's *happened*, nothing's changed! And the Masses, have you checked out your beloved Masses lately? They don't *give* a crap. *(He turns away)* Are you listening? *(Grips his arm urgently)* Are you *listening* to me? I have received your invitation to the Revolution and I send regrets. I'm busy. I've given up on the Twentieth Century in favor of getting through the week. I have decided to feel things where I can get to feel something *back;* got it?

NAT: I was wrong; you're not even smart anymore. So not much changed. So what? You think I don't know this? The proper response to the outrages is still to be outraged. How do you think I got to be eighty-one?

CLARA: *(Her arms outstretched in mock supplication)* Forgive me, Father; I'm not on the barricades anymore! I haven't been arrested for ten years, I'm obviously worthless! If you were talking to me in jail right now, you'd be overjoyed—

NAT: Not overjoyed. *Pleased* maybe . . .

CLARA: Christ, I was the only kid at the Columbia riots whose father showed up to coach! I *still* don't believe it! There you are on the steps of the Administration Building, shouting at the cops, pointing at me—*(Imitating Nat)* Hey Cossacks, look at this one! You can't stop her! *Four* of you—it'll take *four* of you to put her in the wagon!

NAT: It took *six!*

CLARA: *(She suddenly starts to laugh)* My father, my riot manager; God, I still don't believe it . . . a night in the slammer, and you waiting for me in the street when I got out . . . champagne, you had *champagne* . . .

NAT: *(Laughing with her)* It was a graduation. What parent doesn't show up for a graduation?

CLARA: Why the hell am I laughing?

NAT: Because it was funny.

CLARA: *(Shaking her head)* Jesus, what am I going to do with you?

NAT: *(Quietly)* Hello, Rappaport . . . *(No response; he raises his voice)* Hello, Rappaport!

CLARA: I'm not playing.

NAT: Come on, we'll do the "don't slap me on the back" one. You remember.

CLARA: *(Turns away)* I don't.

NAT: Hello, Rappaport!

CLARA: Stop . . .

NAT: Hello, Rappaport; how's the family?

CLARA: *(After a moment, softly)* I'm not Rappaport.

NAT: Hello, Rappaport; how's the shoe business?

CLARA: *(Smiling)* I'm not Rappaport.

NAT: *(Leans toward her, slaps her on the back)* Hello, Rappaport; how the hell are ya?

CLARA: *(Doing the routine)* I'm not Rappaport, and don't slap me on the back!

NAT: Who are *you* to tell me how to say hello to Rappaport?!

(They both laugh. Silence for a moment)

CLARA: *(Turns to him; quietly)* Pop, I have to do something about you.

NAT: No, you don't.

CLARA: Pop—

NAT: At least I'm "Pop" again—

CLARA: You'll get killed. The next time you'll get killed. I dream about it.

NAT: In general, you need better dreams—

CLARA: I want you out of this neighborhood, I want you off the street. I want you safe. I'm determined.

NAT: *(Reaching for walker)* I have an appointment—

CLARA: *(Holds his arm, firmly)* O.K., we have three possibilities, three solutions. You'll have to accept one of them. First, there's living with me in Great Neck; you'll have your own room, your own separate—

NAT: Rejected.

CLARA: Second; Ricky has found a place, not far from us, Maple Hills Senior Residence. I've checked it out; it's the *best* of them— *(Taking Maple Hills book from handbag, showing pages)* really attractive grounds, Pop; this open, sunny, recreation area—

NAT: Rejected.

CLARA: O.K. . . . O.K., there's one more possibility; I'm not crazy about it, but I'm willing to try it for one month. You stay at your place, you do not hide from me, you make yourself available for visits by me or some member of the family once a week. You don't wander the streets, you don't hang around the park; you go out every afternoon to *this* place . . . *(More gently, taking brochure from handbag)* West End Senior Center; I was there this morning, Pop; this is a great place. Hot lunch at noon and then a full afternoon of activities . . .

NAT: *(Puts on bifocals, holds brochure up to his eyes, reading)* "One o'clock; Dr. Gerald Spitzer will present a slide presentation and informative program on home health services; refreshments will be served. Two o'clock: Beginners Bridge with Rose Hagler. Three-fifteen: Arts and Crafts Corner supervised by Ginger Friedman . . ." *(He studies the brochure for a moment)* O.K. . . . we got three possibilities; we got exile in Great Neck, we got Devil's Island, and we got kindergarten. All rejected. *(Hands her back the brochure; rises from bench, opening the walker)* And now, if you'll excuse me . . .

(He starts moving down the path to the right with the walker. We begin to hear the distant sound of the Carousel as he continues down the path)

CLARA: All right, here it is: I'm taking legal action, Pop, I'm going to court. *(Nat stops on the path, his back to her. She remains on the bench)* I saw a lawyer a month ago after the Gristede uprising; I'm prepared. Article Seventy-eight of the Mental Hygiene Law, judicial declaration of incompetency, I'll get Ricky and me authorized as custodians. According to the lawyer I've got more than enough evidence to prove that you are both mentally and physically incapable of managing yourself or your affairs. In addition to a proven history of harassment, impersonation, and assault. *(She turns away; quietly, firmly)* I look at that bandage, I . . . You can hardly see, and with that walker you're a sitting duck. I don't want you hurt, I don't want you dead. Please, don't force me to go to court. If you fight me, you'll lose. If you run away, I'll find you. I'm prepared to let you hate me for this.

(Silence for a moment)

NAT: You're not kidding.

CLARA: I'm not.

(Silence again; only the sound of the distant, gentle, Carousel Music. He moves back to the bench, sits next to her)

NAT: *(Quietly)* Clara, I've got to tell you something. I put it in my papers, a letter for you when I died, you would have known then . . . *(Hesitates a moment, then proceeds gently)* Your mother and I, it was not the liveliest association, but there was great fondness between us. Whatever I tell you now, you must know that. August, Nineteen Thirty-Nine, I'm at the Young Workers' Club on Houston Street; you talked about dialectical materialism and you met girls. It's a Friday night, the day of the Hitler-Stalin Pact; Ribbentrop shakes hands with Molotov on the front page of the *Journal-American* and this woman bursts into tears. Everyone's arguing, discussing, but this woman sits there with her tears falling on the newspaper. This was Ethel, your mother. My heart was hers. Soon we are married; two years later you are born—and during the next ten years those other people. Fine. All is well. Then . . . then comes October, Fifty-Six . . . October Third . . .

(He lapses into silence, turns away)

CLARA: Tell me. What is it?

NAT: I met a girl. I fell in love.

CLARA: You're human, Pop, it happens. There's no need to feel—

NAT: I mean in *love*, Clara. For the first and only time in my life; boom.

CLARA: Don't worry, it's not—

NAT: Clara, she was a *girl*. Twenty-four; I was fifty-five.

CLARA: *(Riveted)* What happened? Where did you meet her?

NAT: It was in the Grand Street Library, second-floor reading room. I'm at the main table, I look up, I see this lovely girl, Hannah, Hannah Pearlman; she's studying a grammar book. She looks up; she *smiles* at me. I can't speak. She goes back to her book. She has a sad look, someone alone. I see a girl, troubled, lost, marks on her hands from the needle-trades. She rises to leave. Someone should speak to her. Can it be me? Can I have the courage . . . ? *(Softly, with love)* I speak. I *speak* to her; and for hours our words come out, and for hours and days after that in her little room on Ludlow Street. It was the most perfect time. She tells me I have saved her from killing herself . . . I saved her just in time . . . just in time, Clara . . . she did not die, she did not die . . . *(Silence for a moment. Then he speaks briskly, as though awakening from a dream)* Well, I'm married to Ethel, nothing can come of it. Four months, it's over. She goes to

live in Israel, a new life. Six months later, a letter . . .
there is a child . . .

CLARA: My God . . .

NAT: A girl . . . And then, every year or two a letter.
Time goes by; I think often of the library and Ludlow
Street. Then silence; there are no letters, never another. Three months ago there's a message for me at
the Socialists' Club: Sergeant Pearlman will be here
at five. Five o'clock, at the door, Sergeant Pearlman is
a girl. In Israel, women, everybody's in the Army for
a year. Well, Sergeant Pearlman . . .

CLARA: Yes . . .

NAT: Sergeant Pearlman is my daughter. Twenty-six, a
face like her mother; a fine face, like a painting. She
herself is an artist; she comes to this country to study
at the Art Students' League and to find me. *(Silence
for a moment)* Here's the point. She has decided to
take care of me; to live with me. That's why I've told
you all this, so you'll know. In December, we leave
for Israel. This is where I will end my days. You see,
there is nothing for you to worry about.

(Silence for a few moments)

CLARA: *(Quietly)* This is . . . this is a lot for me to take
in, all at once. A lot of information . . .

NAT: Not easy, but I'm glad I told you. Better you know
now.

CLARA: I want to meet her.

NAT: You shall.

CLARA: When?

NAT: In two days. Friday. At the Socialists' Club, in the dining room, Friday at lunchtime. I'll bring sandwiches.

CLARA: Good. *(After a moment; softly)* She'll . . . she'll take care of you.

NAT: That's the point.

CLARA: *(Letting it all sink in)* Israel . . .

NAT: Yes, Clara. *(She turns away, trying to cover her emotion. He touches her arm; gently)* Clara, don't be upset. I'll be fine. It's for the best, Clara . . .

(She rises briskly from the bench)

CLARA: Well, at last you've got a daughter who's a soldier.

NAT: Sit. Where are you going?

CLARA: *(Checks watch)* My train. You know, the Siberian Express.

NAT: *(He holds out his hand to her)* They got them every half-hour. Sit a minute.

CLARA: Got to go. See you Friday. *(She moves quickly toward the stone steps at right; near tears)*

NAT: Wait a minute—*(She goes quickly up the steps)* Hey, Rappaport! Hello, Rappaport! *(She exits)* Rappaport, what happened to you? You used to be a tall, fat guy; now you're a—*(She is gone. He shouts)* Rappaport! *(Silence for a moment. He speaks quietly)* Hey, Rappaport . . .

(Silence again. Nat remains quite still on the bench; he strokes his beard nervously, sadly. He suddenly winces, as though aware for the first time of the pain in his hip; shifts position on the bench. Midge, still lying on the stone ledge at far left, lifts the handkerchief off his face)

MIDGE: You made it up.

NAT: *(Softly)* Of course.

MIDGE: You made it all up . . .

NAT: Go back to sleep.

MIDGE: Conned your own kid, that's a sin.

NAT: I did it to save a life. Mine.

MIDGE: *(Sitting up on ledge)* You ain't a nice guy. 'Shamed I even sung a song with you.

NAT: You don't understand. Nursing homes danced in her head; desperate measures were required. *(Grips walker, rising forcefully from bench) You;* you would just go toddling off to Maple Hills.

MIDGE: Wouldn't hustle my own child to save my ass.

NAT: She's not mine anymore. She has become unfamiliar. *(Starts moving Up Left on path, in walker, as though to exit past Midge at ledge)*

MIDGE: Won't get away with it anyway. In two days, she'll—

NAT: *(Continuing forcefully up path)* In two days I'll be in Seattle . . . Hong Kong, Vladivostok, Newark; I'll be where she can't get me.

MIDGE: Seattle; shit, you can't get down*town,* boy.

NAT: I'll be *gone, some*where. When she comes to the Club, I'll be *gone*—

MIDGE: *(Angrily, blocking his path)* And what *she* do? Wait there all day, thinkin' you're dead? *(Nat stops, Midge pointing at him)* What kinda man *are* you? Smart talk and fancy notions, you don't *give* a damn!

NAT: A *letter,* I'll . . . I'll leave a letter for her . . . *(Silence for a moment; he sits on the small bench, upset, confused)* I'll send her a letter; I'll explain the necessity for . . . my behavior . . .

(He trails off into silence, exhausted, at a loss for words; he stares thoughtfully out at the lake)

MIDGE: *(Suddenly looks up at bridge, whispering)* Gilley—

(We have seen the Cowboy enter Up Right on the bridge several moments earlier, strolling halfway across the bridge before Midge notices him; a tall, genial-looking tourist, about thirty-five, he wears an immaculate white Stetson, finely tailored buckskin jacket, and polished boots. He moves politely toward Laurie, stopping a respectful distance from her, peering at the sketch she's been working on; Laurie apparently unaware of him. Nat, lost in his own thoughts, continues to look out at the lake, unaware of Midge and the scene above him)

MIDGE: *(Softly, squinting up at them)* Ain't Gilley; too big . . .

THE COWBOY: *(Smiling, pleasantly, a well-mannered western voice)* Well now, M'am, you sure got that lake just right. Fine work, I'd say. Looks like—

LAURIE: *(Not looking at him)* Fuck off, Cowboy.

THE COWBOY: *(Cordially, tipping his Stetson as though returning her greeting)* Afternoon, M'am.

LAURIE: How did you find me?

THE COWBOY: Natural-born hunter, Miss Laurie. 'Specially rabbits.

LAURIE: Ever tell you how much I hate that bullshit drawl? *(Turns to him)* What is this, Halloween? You haven't been west of Jersey City.

THE COWBOY: Pure accident of birth, M'am. My soul's in Montana where the air is better.

LAURIE: *(Abruptly hands him bank envelope)* See ya later, Cowboy.

(She starts briskly, calmly, across bridge to right)

THE COWBOY: Well, thank you, M'am.

(Opens envelope, starts counting bills inside)

MIDGE: Sure don't *sound* like Ella Mae . . .

THE COWBOY: *(Quietly)* Three hundred and twenty . . . ? *(Laurie quickens her pace across the bridge, almost running)* Three hundred and twenty outa two thousand—

(Laurie races toward the stone steps at right, the Cowboy darts up left, disappearing. Midge quickly grabs Nat, breaking into his reverie, pulling him to his feet)

MIDGE: Come on now—*(Moving Nat into the safety of the shadows at the left of the bridge, whispering)* Bad business . . . bad park business here.

(Laurie races breathlessly down the stone steps toward the Tunnel, an escape—but the Cowboy suddenly emerges from the Tunnel, blocking her path)

THE COWBOY: *(Calmly, evenly)* See the rabbit run. Dirty little rabbit. *(Grips her arms, thrusts her forward toward the bench; she bumps against the bench, dropping her sketchpad. He remains a few steps away; continuing quietly, evenly)* I live in a bad city. What's *happenin'* to this city? City fulla dirty little rabbits. Park fulla junkies; *un*reliable, *dis*honorable junkies . . .

LAURIE: That's all I could—

THE COWBOY: *(Holding up the envelope)* Kept your nose filled and your head happy for a year and a half, and look what you do. Look what you do.

LAURIE: *(Moving toward him)* Sorry, right now that's the best I—

(He slaps her hard across the face with the bank envelope, jerking her head back; then he throws the envelope full of bills to the ground)

NAT: *(From shadows at far left)* What? What happened . . . ?

MIDGE: *(Holding Nat's arm, whispering)* Shhhh . . . stay now.

THE COWBOY: *(Calmly again)* You . . . you got to take me serious. 'Cause you don't take me serious, I don't get my money and you don't get older. *(A moment passes; then he moves past her at the bench, starting toward the Tunnel)* My cash. Tomorrow. Here. Six o'clock.

LAURIE: *(Moving toward him)* Need more time . . . not enough time, I can't—

(In one quick, almost mechanical movement, he turns and hits her sharply in the face, as though correcting an error. She blinks, dizzy from the blow, sits down on the bench, trembling; there is blood on her lip. Nat takes a step forward in his walker, but Midge holds him firmly in the shadows)

THE COWBOY: *(Kneels next to her at the bench; quietly)* Mustn't say "can't," Miss Laurie. Don't say that. You are the little engine that can. I believe in you. *(Takes out his handkerchief, starts quite delicately, carefully, to dab the blood off her mouth)* This gets around, folks'll start thinkin' the Cowboy's got no teeth. Law and order ain't reached these parts; fellah like me got to protect himself, right? *(She nods)* My cash. Tomorrow. Here. Six o'clock. And don't try to hide from me, little rabbit. Don't do that. That would be a mistake. *(She nods. He rises, puts his handkerchief back in his pocket; shakes his head sadly)* Damn town. Damn town's turnin' us all to shit, ain't it? *(Turns, walks briskly into the darkened Tunnel, tipping his hat cordially as he exits)* Afternoon, M'am.

(Laurie kneels down on the ground, sobbing, retrieving the envelope and the scattered bills. Midge moves out of the shadows and quickly toward her, Nat moves slowly toward her in his walker. Midge reaches his hand out tentatively, tenderly touches her shoulder)

MIDGE: You O.K., lady?

LAURIE: *(Tears streaming down her face)* Great. Just great. *(She looks up at them)* Fellahs . . . how ya doin', fellahs?

MIDGE: Here . . . take this. *(Gently hands her his handkerchief; she accepts it, rising to sit on bench. Midge points in the direction of the Cowboy's exit)* That boy; he a dealer, or a shark?

LAURIE: Dealer. But he gave me credit.

MIDGE: Can you get the money? *(She shakes her head hopelessly. He nods)* Uh-huh. What I heard, lady, you best get outa town; fast and far.

LAURIE: I was just gettin' it together . . . straightening out, Mister . . . *(Shaking with sobs, opening sketchpad, showing him the pages)* Art school, I started art school, see . . .

MIDGE: *(Softly, touching her shoulder)* Outa town, chil'; fast and far.

LAURIE: These guys, you don't get away; they got branch offices, man, they got chain stores . . .

NAT: She's right. *(Parks his walker next to the bench)* Other measures are called for. *(He sits next to her)* Tell me, Miss; two days from now, Friday, what are you doing for lunch on Friday?

LAURIE: *(Quietly, trembling)* Friday . . . ? Jesus, looks like Friday I'll be in the hospital. Or dead maybe . . . or dead . . .

NAT: *(His arm around her; gently, firmly)* No, you won't be in the hospital. I promise you. And you will not die . . . you will not die.

(Blackout. In the darkness we hear the sound of the Carousel Band-Organ playing "The Sidewalks of New York"; the music building gradually louder in the darkness, reaching a peak and then slowly fading as the lights come up.

It is six o'clock, the evening of the next day. Midge and Nat are alone on the path, seated on the center bench. Nat wears dark sunglasses, a white scarf, and an old but stylish Homburg, his cane at his side, his walker folded and hidden behind the bench. He looks serious and elegant. Midge wears an old suit-jacket instead of his usual sweater, and a hat that he had once considered fashionable. The bridge lampposts are lit above; the dark shadows of early evening gather in the Tunnel and along the path. Midge glances anxiously up and down the path. He lights a cigarette, inhales, coughs. Silence for a few moments)

NAT: Time, please.

MIDGE: *(Takes out pocketwatch, holds it up against his bifocals)* Ten to six.

NAT: Good. Say my name again.

MIDGE: I got it, I got it; you keep—

NAT: Say the name.

MIDGE: Donatto.

NAT: The whole name.

MIDGE: Anthony Donatto.

NAT: Better known as?

MIDGE: *(Impatiently)* Tony the Cane. O.K.? Now will
ya—

NAT: Tony the Cane Donatto. Good. O.K., *your* name.

MIDGE: I—

NAT: Your name.

MIDGE: *(With a sigh of resignation)* Kansas City Jack.

NAT: *Missouri* Jack, *Missouri* Jack. *See*, it's lucky I
asked.

MIDGE: Missouri Jack, Kansas City Jack, what the hell's
the *difference?* He ain't even gonna ask me.

NAT: It could come *up.* In these matters details are
very important. Details is the whole game, believe
me. What time is it?

MIDGE: I just told—

NAT: Missouri Jack is better than Kansas City Jack. Has
a sound to it. Music. I know these things. Details is
everything. You should introduce yourself to him.

MIDGE: Nossir, *nossir;* do what I *said* I'd do and that's *it.*
Don't even like doin' *that* much. Dicey deal here, say
the least— *(Starts to cough, indicates cigarette)*

Looka me, ain't had a cigarette thirty-two years, July; you got me smokin' again. *(Pointing at him)* O.K., promised that po' girl I'd help her out, but I ain't hangin' around here a second longer'n I have to. You a time-bomb, Mister, I hear you tickin'.

NAT: I ask you to look at the record, sir! I ask you to look at the *harm* I've done you! Gilley did not return yesterday as I predicted and he did not come today. No more payoffs; correct?

MIDGE: O.K., so far he—

NAT: And your job—has anybody there *mentioned* firing you since I dealt with Danforth? Do you still have your home?

MIDGE: Yeah, well, O.K., so far they—

NAT: And today a few minutes of your time to help the victim of Gene Autry; the woman requires our aid. He comes here, you go up to him, you say "excuse me, my boss wants to see you," you send him over to me and you're *done;* finished.

MIDGE: You bet; then I *split,* that's *it.* Go home, hear about it on the TV. *(Shaking his head mournfully)* Still don't see why you even need me to—

NAT: *Details, details;* gives him the feeling I've got a staff, an organization. It fills in the picture. Details are crucial. I know my business. What time is it? *(Midge sighs, takes out his pocketwatch. Nat turns, squinting into the Tunnel)* Never mind; he's here. On the button.

(Midge turns sharply as the Cowboy emerges from the darkened Tunnel. Nat adjusts his Homburg, crosses his legs, leans back on the bench. The Cowboy walks down to the ledge at far left, glances about, then looks solemnly up at the bridge. After a few moments he sits down at the edge of the ledge, takes off his Stetson, starts cleaning it carefully with a small brush, waiting. Midge remains quite still on the bench, looking out at the lake. Silence for a few moments)

NAT: *(Whispering)* Now. *(Midge continues to look out at the lake. Nat whispers again)* Now, Carter.

(Midge rises, buttons his jacket, straightens his hat, preparing himself; then crosses to within six feet of the Cowboy. The Cowboy is looking away from him, watching the path at left)

MIDGE: *(Barely audible)* Excuse me, my boss wants to see you. *(No response. He speaks a bit louder)* Excuse me, Mister . . . my boss wants to see you.

THE COWBOY: *(Turns to Midge)* You talkin' to *me*, partner?

MIDGE: Yeah. *(Points behind him)* My boss over there, he wants to see you.

THE COWBOY: Your boss?

MIDGE: Yeah, I'm on his staff. He wants to see you.

THE COWBOY: Who the hell're you?

MIDGE: Me? I'm nobody. I'm on the staff.

THE COWBOY: *(Leans toward him)* What do you want with me? Who are you?

MIDGE: I'm . . . I'm Missouri Jack.

THE COWBOY: Missouri Jack. Sounds familiar. You ever—

MIDGE: You don't know me. I'm nobody.

THE COWBOY: Nobody?

MIDGE: Yeah, definitely. Nobody at all; believe me. *(The Cowboy shrugs, turns away)* Him, over there, he's somebody. He wants to see you.

THE COWBOY: I'm busy.

MIDGE: He's the boss. Donatto. Tony Donatto.

THE COWBOY: Great. I'm busy.

(He leans back on the ledge, looking the other way, ignoring Midge, watching the path)

MIDGE: O.K. then, guess I'll be on my way. *(He turns, starts walking briskly toward the stone steps at far right)* Yeah, gotta be gettin' along now. Nice meetin' you, pleasure talkin' to you . . .

NAT: *(To Cowboy, loudly)* Hey, Tom Mix. *(The Cowboy turns; Nat pats the bench)* You, Roy Rogers, over here.

THE COWBOY: What do *you* want?

NAT: I want not to shout. Come here. *(No response. Midge quickens his pace up the steps)* Laurie Douglas, two thousand dollars.

THE COWBOY: What—

NAT: You know the name? You know the sum? *(Pats bench)* Here. We'll talk.

(The Cowboy starts toward him. Midge stops in the shadows halfway up the steps, turns, curious, watching them at a safe distance. Nat will remain aloof behind his sunglasses, seldom facing the Cowboy, never raising his voice)

THE COWBOY: *(Approaching bench)* What *about* Laurie Douglas? Who are you?

NAT: I am Donatto. Sit.

THE COWBOY: Look, if that junkie bimbo thinks she can—

NAT: The junkie bimbo is my daughter. Sit.

THE COWBOY: She's got a father, huh? *(Sits)* Thought things like her just accumulated.

NAT: *(Taking old silver case from jacket, removing small cigar)* Not that kind of father. Another kind of father. I have many daughters, many sons. In my family there are many children. I am Donatto.

(He lights the cigar. The Cowboy studies him)

THE COWBOY: I never heard of—

NAT: On your level, probably not. *(Patting the Cowboy's knee)* A lot of you new boys don't know. I fill you in. My people, we work out of Phoenix. We take commands from Nazzaro, Los Angeles; Capetti, New Orleans . . . *(No response; Nat leans toward him)* *Capetti*, New Orleans . . . *(Turns to Midge)* Jack, he doesn't know Capetti, New Orleans . . . *(Nat chuckles heartily, Midge stares blankly back at him; Nat turns to the Cowboy again)* Capetti will be amused by you. I am not Capetti, many years ago, he gives us our name—I talk of the old days now, the good days—he calls us, me and Jack, "The Travel Agents." This is because we arrange for trips to the place of no return. You understand?

THE COWBOY: *(Sharply, snapping his fingers)* Let's get *to* it, pal, there's some *bucks* owed me—

NAT: *(Covers the Cowboy's snapping fingers with his hand, gently)* Please don't do that, it upsets me. We will speak of your problem now. The girl, Laurie; I am not pleased with her. A two-grand marker for drugs, she brings shame on my house. She says she is slapped, threatened. I am unhappy with this. It is not for you to deal with her. She is of my family. Forget the girl; you never met her. Forget, Cowboy, or you yourself become a memory.

THE COWBOY: *(Smiles, leans back on bench)* You tryin' t'tell me that two old guys like you—

NAT: Of course not. We don't touch people like you; we have *people* who touch people like you. I pick up a phone, you disappear. I make a call, they find you floating. Yes, we are old now, the Travel Agents; many years since we did our own work. In Fifty-Four, our last active year . . . *(Turns to Midge)* How many floating, Jack? *(Silence. Midge stares blankly back at him)* He doesn't remember either. I think if we count Schwartzman, it was fourteen—

THE COWBOY: *(Leaning very close to him)* Don't like the sound of this, hoss; it does not ring right in the ear.

NAT: Don't you understand? Missouri and me, we fly here personally from Phoenix last night to speak to you—

THE COWBOY: If you just came in from Phoenix, what were you doing here yesterday?

NAT: Yesterday? What're you—

THE COWBOY: And the day before that. Seen you here two days runnin'.

NAT: You . . . you are mistaken—

(Midge starts to retreat up the steps toward the exit)

THE COWBOY: *(Lifts walker up from behind bench)* Had this with you yesterday. I got an antenna picks up all channels, Dad; helps me not to wake up dead.

NAT: I advise you to call your people, check the name—

THE COWBOY: Game's over, stop it—

NAT: Call them now—

THE COWBOY: Please don't continue this. I'm gettin' depressed—

NAT: You are making a serious mistake, a very serious—

THE COWBOY: *Please* don't do this—*(He throws the walker clattering to the ground) Hate* bein' played foolish; *hate* it. First she cons me, then she gets two old creeps to front for her. Don't *like* it. *(Pacing behind bench)* City gone rotten, shills like you; Big Apple rottin' away . . . *(Nat starts to rise; the Cowboy pulls him sharply back down onto the bench)* This is hurtin' me. Makin' me *feel* bad. *(Pulls off Nat's sunglasses)* Who *are* you, man? *(Yanks off his Homburg)* What's the deal? Where is she?

NAT: *(Quietly)* A . . . a note was left with my attorney this morning. If I do not return by seven, they will send people here. His card— *(Hands him business card)*

THE COWBOY: *(Crushing the card in his hand)* You're out of aces, friend. Where's she hidin'? Where's she at?

NAT: I am not at liberty to—

THE COWBOY: *(Grips Nat's scarf, pulls him close)* Run a street business. Lookin' bad on the street, girl's makin' me look like shit on the street. Got folks *laughin'* at me. *(Gives him one fierce shake)* You got to take me *serious* now. You got to tell me where she's *at.*

NAT: *(Quietly)* Allow me to introduce myself; I . . . I'm . . .

(The Cowboy pulls the scarf tighter around Nat's neck, like a kind of noose, shaking him violently now, shouting)

THE COWBOY: You in harm's way, Dad, you in harm's *way* now! Got to *tell* me, got to *tell* me! Gonna rock you till the *words* come out— *(Shaking him fiercely, continuously, rhythmically, Nat halfway off the bench now, almost falling to the ground)* Rock you, *rock* you, *rock* you—

MIDGE: *(Taking a step down the stairs)* Leave him be! Leave him *be* now!

THE COWBOY: *(Continues shaking Nat)* Rock you, *rock* you—

MIDGE: Leave the man be! Leave him go else I get a cop!

THE COWBOY: *(Turns, still holding Nat)* Well now, it's Mr. Nobody . . .

MIDGE: *(Retreating a step)* You . . . you go away, you leave him be else I get a cop. *(Pointing Up Right, trembling)* Cop right near—cop car at the boathouse this hour, right near.

THE COWBOY: That case you don't *move,* little man, you stay right *there* . . .

(Midge hesitates; then starts up the stairs)

THE COWBOY: I ask you not to go, little man . . .

(Midge continues up the stairs as quickly as he can; The Cowboy lets go of Nat, letting him fall to the ground, starts toward the stairs)

THE COWBOY: Askin' you to *stop,* buddy; stop right there—

(Midge stops on the stairs, his back to the Cowboy. The Cowboy continues toward the base of the stairs; Midge turns, holding Gilley's unsheathed hunting knife high in the air; the large blade glistens. The Cowboy stops; backs up a bit toward the Tunnel. The knife is shaking; Midge grips the handle with both hands to steady it)

THE COWBOY: *(Tips back his Stetson)* Well now, well now . . . what do we got here?

MIDGE: We got a crazy old man with a knife.

THE COWBOY: Crazy ol' man, you can't even see me.

MIDGE: *(Still trembling)* See a blue shadow with a hat on it. Come close enough, I stick you. *(A step forward, thrusting knife)* I swear I stick you, boy.

(The Cowboy starts retreating back toward the Tunnel; smiles, tips his hat, as though gracefully admitting defeat)

THE COWBOY: Afternoon, Jack.

(He turns as though exiting into the Tunnel; it would appear to Midge that the Cowboy is leaving, but we can see that he has merely ducked into the shadows within the Tunnel, at right, where he waits for Midge. Midge continues toward the Tunnel, his courage and pride building, his knife raised high)

NAT: *(From the ground, whispering)* Get away, Carter . . . get away . . .

MIDGE: *(Moving into Tunnel, shouting)* Now *you* the one goes away, *you* the one does the leavin', cowboy; this here's *my* spot . . . *(Continuing into Tunnel, unaware that the Cowboy is hidden just behind him in the shadows of the Tunnel Archway)* Mess with me, I peel you like an apple! Sliced Cowboy comin' up! Cowboy Salad to go—

(The Cowboy moves suddenly out of the shadows behind Midge—we see the sharp, violent thrust of the Cowboy's hand as he grabs Midge's shoulder—

Blackout; the sudden loud, pulsing rhythm of the Ca-
rousel Band-Organ playing "Springtime in the Rock-
ies." The powerful sound of the Band-Organ continues
in the darkness for a few moments, and then the red-
orange colors of autumn gradually light up the sky
behind the bridge, leaving the downstage area in dark-
ness and the bridge and the Archway in stark silhou-
ette. Leaves fall against the red-orange sky; the Carou-
sel Music continuing powerfully for several moments
and then slowly fading into the distant, more delicate
melody of "The Queen City March" as the rest of the
lights come up.

It is twelve days later, a cloudy autumn morning,
eleven o'clock. Nat is alone on the path, seated at the far
left end of the bench. He wears his bifocals, a thick
woolen scarf, and a faded winter coat; his walker is
folded at his side, his briefcase nowhere in sight. He
remains quite still, staring rather listlessly out at the
lake; from time to time he shivers slightly in the Octo-
ber breeze, holds the scarf up closer about his neck. He
seems fragile, older—or rather he seems to be his own
age, very much like any old man whiling away his
morning on a park bench. Several moments pass. A few
autumn leaves drift lazily down onto the path. Silence
except for the now quite distant and gentle sound of the
Carousel Music. After a while Nat reaches into his
jacket pocket, takes out the West End Senior Center
brochure, holds it up to his bifocals, studying it. Several
more moments pass.

We see Midge appear in the darkened Tunnel; he is
moving slowly and carefully through the Tunnel with
the aid of a "quad-cane"—a cane with four aluminum

rubber-tipped legs at its base. It takes him several moments to reach the bench; he crosses in front of Nat, ignoring him, sits at the far right end of the bench, opens his copy of The Sporting News, *starts to read. The Carousel Music fades out. Silence for a few moments. Nat turns, leans toward Midge)*

MIDGE: *(Quietly)* Don't say a word.

NAT: *(After a moment)* I was only—

MIDGE: Not a word, please.

(Silence again. Midge continues to read his newspaper)

NAT: I was only going to say that, quite frankly, I have missed you, Carter.

MIDGE: O.K., now you said it.

NAT: *(After a moment)* I would also like to express my delight at your safe return from the hospital. I only regret that you did not allow me into your room to visit you.

MIDGE: Ain't lettin' *you* in there—shit, tell 'em you're a doctor, start loppin' off pieces of my foot. Had twelve beautiful days an' nights without you.

NAT: Quite right. I don't blame you.

MIDGE: Told 'em, don't let him in what*ever* he says—he tell you he the head of the hospital, tell you he invented *novocaine*, you don't let him in.

NAT: I certainly don't blame you. The fact is I've stopped doing that.

MIDGE: Yeah, *sure*—

NAT: It's true. Since the Cowboy—an episode during which, may I say, you behaved magnificently; not since General Custer has there been such behavior— since that time I have been only myself. That Friday, Clara comes lunchtime to the Socialists' Club; I tell her the truth. She comes, there are tears in her eyes, I decide to tell her the truth. I will admit I was helped in this decision by the fact that the girl, Laurie, did not show up. *(He turns away, quietly)* I could have covered, another story, my heart wasn't in it. My mouth, a dangerous mouth; it makes you Missouri Jack and almost kills you; makes an Israeli family and breaks my daughter's heart. I have retired my mouth.

MIDGE: *(Still looking away, bitterly)* Yeah, well, long's we talkin' *mouth* damage, boy—lawyer for the Tenants' Committee found out there ain't no HURTS-FOE; I'm outa my *job* now. Yeah, movin' me and the Erie City out in four weeks. No extra severance neither. Danforth come to the hospital to tell me personal; bring me a basket of fruit. Now 'stead of my Christmas cash I got six fancy pears wrapped in silver paper.

NAT: I . . . I deeply regret—

MIDGE: 'Sides which, look what you done to Laurie. How you expect her to show up? Said you'd help her with that Cowboy; now she's in worse trouble than ever. *(Bangs his quad-cane on the ground)* 'Sides which, there ain't one good hip left on this bench now. And long's we keepin' score here, what happened to Gilley? Tell me the truth; Gilley's *back*, ain't he?

NAT: *(After a moment)* Yes. *(Quietly)* He charges six dollars now.

MIDGE: So seems to me you pretty much come up "O" for Five on the whole series here.

NAT: Please, I assure you, my wounds require no further salt . . .

MIDGE: 'Nother thing—I ain't no General Custer. Way I heard it, the General got wiped out. Well, not *this* boy. Shit, wasn't for a lucky left jab I near blew that Cowboy away. *(Takes a small piece of buckskin fringe from his pocket)* See this? Small piece of that Cowboy is what it is. His jacket, anyways. Near took a good slice outa that boy, 'fore he dropped me. *(Leans back on bench, smiling)* Know what I seen in the hospital every night, fronta my bed? I seen that Cowboy's eyes, them scared eyes, them big chicken eyes when my weapon come out. That was one, surprised, frozen-solid, near-shitless Cowboy. Dude didn't know *what* happened. Dude figured he had me on the ropes, out come my weapon and he turn *stone*. Lord, even eyes like mine I seen *his* eyes, they got *that* big lookin' at me. Yeah, yeah, he seen *me*, all right, he *seen* me; gonna be a while 'fore he mess with

this alley cat again. *(Studying the piece of buckskin)*
Must be a way to frame a thing like this . . .

*(Sound of the distant Carousel Band-Organ playing
"Sidewalks of New York"; Nat looks up, realizing what
time it must be)*

NAT: *(Starts to rise, using bench for support)* Unfortu-
nately, I must leave now . . .

MIDGE: *(Turns to him, smiles)* Best news I heard all
day.

NAT: I am expected at the Senior Center at noon. The
day begins at noon there. I must be prompt; Clara
checks up. *(Unfolding the walker)* Also weekends in
Great Neck. I am seldom in the park anymore.

MIDGE: *(Returns to his newspaper)* News is gettin' better and better . . .

NAT: *(Steps inside of walker, his hands on the rails)*
The hospital said you just got out, I came today on the
chance of seeing you. I felt I owed you an apology;
also the truth. My name is Nat Moyer; this is my
actual name. I was a few years with the Fur Workers'
Union, this was true, but when Ben Gold lost power
they let me go. I was then for forty-one years a waiter
at Deitz's Dairy Restaurant on Houston Street; that's
all, a waiter. I was retired at age seventy-three; they
said they would have kept me on except I talked too
much, annoyed the customers. I presently reside, and
have for some time, at the Amsterdam Hotel; here
my main occupation is learning more things about

tuna fish than God ever intended. In other words, whatever has been said previously, I was, and am now, no one. No one at all. This is the truth. Goodbye and good luck to you and your knife. *(He starts moving slowly down the path with his walker toward the exit at left)* Better get going to the Center. At twelve guest speaker Jerome Cooper will lecture on "Timely Issues for the Aging"; refreshments will be served to anyone who's alive at the end . . .

MIDGE: *(Quietly, shaking his head)* Shit, man, you *still* can't tell the truth.

NAT: *(Continues moving away)* That was the truth.

MIDGE: Damn it, tell me the truth.

NAT: I *told* you the truth. That's what I was, that's all—

MIDGE: *(Angrily, slapping the bench)* No, you wasn't a waiter. What was you really?

NAT: I was a waiter . . .

MIDGE: *(Shouting angrily)* You wasn't just a waiter, you was *more* than that! Tell me the truth, damn it—

NAT: *(He stops on the path; shouts)* I was a *waiter,* that's it! *(Silence for a moment; then he continues down the path. He stops after a few steps; silence again. Then, quietly)* Except, of course, for a brief time in the motion picture industry.

MIDGE: You mean the movies?

NAT: Well, *you* call it the movies; *we* call it the motion picture industry.

MIDGE: What kinda job you have there?

NAT: A job? What I did you couldn't call a job. You see, I was, briefly, a mogul.

MIDGE: Mogul; yeah, I hearda that. Ain't that some kinda Rabbi or somethin'?

NAT: In a manner of speaking, yes. *(Moving toward Midge at bench)* A sort of motion picture rabbi, you might say. One who leads, instructs, inspires; that's a mogul. It's the early Fifties, Blacklisting, the Red scare, terror reigns, the industry is frozen. Nobody can make a move. It's colleague against colleague, brother against brother. I had written a few articles for the papers, some theories on the subject. Suddenly, they call me, they fly me there—boom, I'm a mogul. *(Sitting on bench)* The industry needs answers. What should I do?

MIDGE: *(Leans toward him, intently)* What did you do?

NAT: Well, that's a long story . . . a long and complicated story . . .

(He crosses his legs, leans back on the bench, about to launch into his story, the Carousel Music building loudly as . . .

THE CURTAIN FALLS)